Canvas Work

By the same author

The Care and Repair of Sails

The Complete Crossword Companion

Offshore Crew

Night Intruder

Practical Pilotage

Sails

Small Boat Sails

Teach Your Child About Sailing

Out in Front (sailing film by ICI Fibres) Technical Adviser

Canvas Work

by

Jeremy Howard-Williams

S

**SHERIDAN
HOUSE**

First published in the United States of America 1993 by
Sheridan House Inc.
145 Palisade Street
Dobbs Ferry, NY 10522

Reprinted 1995

Library of Congress Cataloging-in-Publication Data
Howard-Williams, Jeremy, 1922-
Canvas Work/Jeremy Howard-Williams.
   p,   cm.
Includes bibliographical references and index.
ISBN 0-924486-60-0 (pbk.) $11.95
1. Canvas. 2. Marine canvas work. 3. Textile crafts. I. Title.
TT715.H69 1993
746 -- dc20   93-24428
                                                                          CIP

Printed in Great Britain

ISBN 0-924486-60-0

All illustrations by Jeremy Howard-Williams except where otherwise indicated and Fig 3.3 by Keith Jordan.

Contents

List of Tables

List of Figures

Introduction

This book embraces all the kinds of canvas work which you would expect to find on a boat, such as hatch covers, bunk leecloths and sail coats. But it also includes such items as will be of help to the camper, the gardener and the farm worker. The word **canvas** covers all forms of fabric, woven and film alike, which may be used for these applications; leather is only considered where it is used for reinforcing purposes. Canvas made either of natural or of synthetic fibres is dealt with because the principles of cutting and sewing remain the same (with the single significant advantage to man-made fibres that the cloth may be cut and sealed in one hot-iron process).

The common theme which runs through the book is one of strength. By the very nature of their use, most of the items discussed get some pretty rough treatment, so their materials (and the equipment used to work them) have to be on the robust side. The spin-off from this is that some of them don't need workmanship of dressmaking standards.

The main difference with which we need to concern ourselves is whether the end product should be waterproof or not. Man-made fibres are usually almost unaffected by water, so that any slackness in the weave remains the same in rain, spray or shine, thus allowing leaks through the cloth. If it needs to be waterproof, synthetic material has to be treated by the addition of vinyl or resins to one or both sides (where they may be more or less successful in penetrating the mesh of the weave). The very success of this process brings other problems (wouldn't you know it?); these are concerned with the condensation which occurs if air circulation is restricted and the cloth cannot 'breathe'. Natural fibres, on the other hand, tend to swell when moistened, which closes the gap between the cross threads of a closely woven cloth, thus blocking the passage of further water. When natural fabric dries out, the threads return to normal and allow the canvas to breathe again, so that condensation is less. This quality is so desirable in sail covers and the like, that successful part-proofing of synthetic cloth such as acrylic can now ensure a similar dual function, thus avoiding the disadvantages of mildew and rot attendant on cotton and flax products when they are stored damp. The chapter on materials enlarges on the weakening suffered by some synthetics which are subjected to prolonged sunlight (ultraviolet rays) or industrial smoke, and this is another factor which affects choice of material – man-made or natural.

It is hoped that this book will advise on materials and manufacture of most canvas goods which you may want to make. If you don't find the precise item you need among the suggestions and ideas offered, you should find enough basic information to enable you to improvise for yourself.

The most important piece of advice which I can give the aspiring amateur is, 'Have a go'. You'll never get anywhere by hanging back and wondering whether you have the skills. If a seventeen-year-old apprentice can pick up canvas work in a short time, let us hope that you can do so as well. Of course you will not master the entire craft in a matter of days, but you may surprise yourself, and you will certainly find that you can make entirely acceptable jobs of some of the simpler items. The basic equipment of sewing palm, waxed twine, needles and a piece of old canvas will cost you less than dinner for one at a restaurant, so forego an evening out and set yourself up. Then start to make friends with your palm, until the basic sewing process, as described early in the book, is almost second nature. Now select one of the simpler jobs to complete, and get stuck in. It may be best to start on something which can be finished in one weekend, even by a beginner; try patching an old hatch cover or truck tarpaulin, or else make something simple without any shaping, such as bunk leecloths or a sea cook's webbing harness. Perhaps you will then be encouraged to venture further and try your hand on a fitted cover of some kind, perhaps a sail coat.

All this presupposes that you have a suitable environment to work in. The professional will have a special bench and a clean loft; you have to sort out some space where you can make a bit of a mess, and leave it *in situ* when you are called away to attend to lesser activities such as eating, sleeping and working. In summer a garage can be useful, or an attic if it has a floor and some power (why do you think it is also called a loft?); but in winter you may have to take over the dining room, a spare bedroom, or even one end of the living room (and you'll need to be ready to tidy everything away if unexpected visitors call). A first step might be to go out and buy a wooden kitchen stool, and screw on an attached work tray like the one shown in Fig. 1.10, to keep your bits and pieces tidy and to hand.

As usual, I have received much kindness and help from the various people whom I have approached while writing this book, their guidance has been invaluable, and any remaining errors are mine alone. Special mention should be made of the following, with pride of place going to Mrs Joan Hurl of W.G. Lucas & Son (use of fabrics in general, and freedom of the Lucas store of catalogues and fact sheets), Jonathan Barnbrook also of W.G. Lucas (acrylics, polyethelene and cotton), Bainbridge Aquabatten (polyester cloth and thread), Bowmer-Bond Narrow Fabrics Ltd (tape and webbing), Bob Reilly of Bruce Banks Sails (hand twine), J. & P. Coats Ltd (thread), Glanmire Industries Ltd (Scotchgard), Lows of Dundee Ltd (PVC coated polyester), Henry Milward & Sons (needles), James Pearsall & Co. Ltd (thread), Sea-Sure Ltd (hand swager), and last but not least, Singer Consumer Products (sewing machines).

Many proprietory names and registered trade marks have passed into the language as everyday terms. Where such words have been knowingly used in this book, the first mention in the text has been indicated by the symbol® . Unwitting inclusion of further unidentified registered trade marks does not imply that they have necessarily acquired a general significance in the legal sense, and I apologise for not noting them, as I also do for any wrong attribution which I may have made. Substantiated objections will be rectified in any future printing of this work if they are made with due notice.

There is much satisfaction to be achieved from producing your own canvas work, not to mention the financial saving involved. Here's to straight and even stitching.

J.H-W.
Warsash 1988

1 The Tools

There are canvas working tools and canvas working tools. If you intend merely to dabble in the craft, then you only need the minimum kit. If, however, you hope to be reasonably aggressive, and to make something worthwhile, then you will want to consider some of the following.

Hand Work

Apron

If any serious hand work is to be undertaken, a lap apron of stiff material will be useful, if not essential. This will prevent the needle from sticking into your clothes or, worse still, your thighs.

Fig. 1.1 shows representative sizes, but use your kitchen or barbecue apron as a pattern; this need have no shaping, except that a curve as shown in dashed outline will make it fit better under the arms. The edges need not be hemmed if the material is synthetic, but hems make a better-looking job and they will give you some useful sewing practice. A pocket is a useful adjunct; the felt flap is for spare needles, and the ring is for lengths of twine, hooks or any general use.

Needles

Hand sewing needles come in many shapes and sizes. We shall be using principally the sailmaker's needle, but there will also be a need for the domestic varieties.

Sailmaker's needles   These are triangular in shape, in order to force a way between the weave, leaving a large enough hole to receive the thread, doubled through the eye; there is a short round barrel between the blade and the eye; Fig. 1.2(a). It is important to remember that they may *look* stainless when bought, but they are not. Rust makes needles unnecessarily difficult to use, not to say impossible, so store them in an oiled rag or small bottle with a drop or two (not more) of oil or vaseline jelly in it; wipe clean before use if you don't want to stain the product (there is a prophylactic paper called Ban-Rust, but I have no experience of it). Sailmaker's needles are sized so that their round barrel sections conform with the standard wire gauge. The starred sizes in Table 1 below should be adequate to start with (your local sailmaker will almost certainly sell them to you). In coarse cloth, the smaller sizes break fairly easily so be prepared with spares.

Size	Length		Use
	Nominal	Actual	
4-8	6-4½ in		Extra large
9	4 in	3.9 in	Heaviest roping
10	3¾ in	3.7 in	
11	3½ in	3.4 in	
*12	3¼ in	3.2 in	Heavy canvas or roping
13	3 in	3.0 in	
*14	2¾ in	2.9 in	Medium canvas or
14½	2⅝ in	2.8 in	light roping
15	2½ in	2.7 in	
*16	2⅜ in	2.6 in	Light canvas
17	2¼ in	2.5 in	
*18	2⅛ in	2.4 in	Light nylon
19	2 in	2.3 in	

Table 1. *Hand-sewing needles. Starred sizes are recommended for basic kit. Dull the point of one of your size 12's before roping, if you want to avoid catching too many loose strands as you sew between the lay.*

Packing needles   These are longer than sailmaker's needles, and have a slightly curved blade to allow sewing from one side of a coarse material, such as hessian or burlap, when it is stretched taut; see Fig. 1.2(b). Not an essential item, and you may safely wait until the need arises.

Upholstery needles   These are entirely semi-circular and come in a variety of sizes. As the name implies, they are used for upholstery purposes (they are sometimes also called glover's needles), and for bunk cushions and soft canvas, etc; Fig. 1.2(c). Because they are not general use items, you will be advised to wait until you need one before buying it – unless you spot one of the handy cards of assorted needles made by Henry Milward & Sons (of Studley, Warwickshire, B80 7AS, England; their ref A.1222).

Domestic needles   A small needle from the domestic sewing box will find a use when dealing with light nylon; if you have poor eyesight, a *darning needle* has a large eye (and is thus easier to thread); Fig. 1.2(d). What is sometimes called a *tapestry needle* (it has a fairly stout body, a blunt

Fig. 1.1 Apron

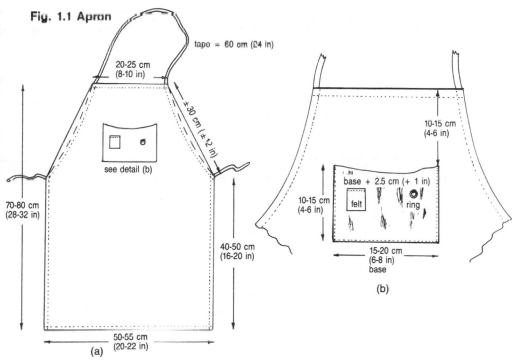

tapo = 60 cm (24 in)

20-25 cm
(8-10 in)

± 30 cm (± 12 in)

see detail (b)

70-80 cm
(28-32 in)

40-50 cm
(16-20 in)

50-55 cm
(20-22 in)

(a)

10-15 cm
(4-6 in)

base + 2.5 cm (+ 1 in)

felt

ring

10-15 cm
(4-6 in)

15-20 cm
(6-8 in)
base

(b)

A stout canvas of polyester or heavy cotton will provide best protection. Patches and pockets may be improvised at will.

Fig. 1.2 Needles

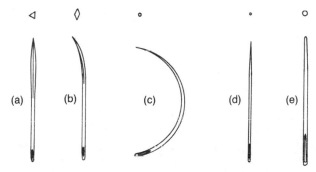

(a)   (b)   (c)   (d)   (e)

In the illustration, the section of each needle is shown above it.
(a)   The sailmaker's needle has a triangular blade, to make a hole large enough to pass the doubled twine;
(b)   Packing needle (works heavy canvas from one side only);
(c)   Upholstery needle (works light canvas from one side only);
(d)   Darning needle (large eye);
(e)   Tapestry needle (large eye and blunt point make it a good bodkin).

point and a very large eye) can be useful as a bodkin for threading a drawstring or messenger; Fig. 1.2(e). If you want a similar one, but with a sharp point, it is called a *chenille needle*.

Sewing palm

A sewing palm is the badge of office of the artisan. If you only propose to dabble in sailmaking or canvas work, then by all means buy the first palm which presents itself. If, however, you want to be a bit more serious, it is worth taking some time over its selection. William Smith of Redditch list no fewer than sixteen different palms in their catalogue.

Palms may be broadly divided into *roping palms* and *seaming palms*. The former are usually more substantial than the latter, with a deep set needle plate (to accommodate the rather longer needle of size 12 and larger), and an extended thumb guard (round which to wind the twine to heave each stitch tight). Seaming palms are lighter in construction, and possibly softer and quicker to adapt to your hand; Fig. 1.3. A good one is solidly built, with a substantial pigskin reinforcement round the needle plate, and is more properly termed a *sailmaker's palm*. Beware of the cheap palms which are sometimes offered as seaming or *sailor's palms* (some of them even made of plastic rather than leather). The perfectionist will learn the rudiments on a cheap seaming palm and, when he or she knows what's what, will select the ultimate weapon and allow it time to shape itself to the hand under the influence of sweat and usage. Get a good one and allow it time for this process of adjustment – and then treasure it. Left-handed palms can be obtained by the persistent, but I am told that their use is unusual, even by left-handers (but my informant was right-handed).

Fig. 1.3 Sailmaker's palm

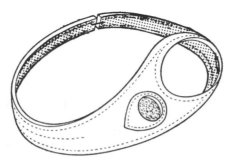

The sailmaker's sewing palm does not have the raised thumb piece and large needle plate of the professional's roping palm.

Hand twine

Hand sewing uses a heavier thread than a machine, and it is usually called twine rather than thread. Only when you are sewing cotton or flax cloth should you consider using cotton hand twine for boat covers, awnings, etc., and even then there are many points in favour of polyester. It should be waxed to prevent the strands unravelling and to hold the stitches in place; ready-waxed twine is available on spools or cops, or it may be treated by drawing it two or three times across a cake of beeswax. Barbour Threads of Northern Ireland make a conventional twisted multi-filament twine, and there is also a braided flat pre-waxed hand twine sold by Bainbridge Aquabatten. Most polyester twine these days is not only prewaxed, but also inhibited against attack by the ultraviolet rays of the sun; the heavy weights we are considering are therefore largely unaffected save by the most prolonged exposure.

In England, conventional multi-filament thread for hand sewing is graded in pounds breaking strain (in even numbers from 2–10). The USA has a grading based on the Tex system, with figures using a V-prefix running from low for light to high for heavy. Flat braided twine is sold by its width, being $^1/_{16}$ and $^1/_8$ inch.

If you intend any prolonged work, buy your twine economically on a large cop, rather than the dinky spool sold in many chandleries (your sailmaker should be able to help). You will need one fairly heavy (for roping and heavy canvas), one medium (for general work), and some machine thread (for any hand work on nylon). Table 2 gives some recommended sizes.

Canvas	Conventional twisted multi-filament twine		Braided flat twine	Hand needle
	lb	USA	width	size
Heavy	8–10	V.462	$^1/_8$ in	12
Medium	4–6	V.346	$^1/_{16}$ in	14–16
Light	2	V.69	–	18

Table 2. *Recommended twine and needle sizes for use in canvas cover work.*

Beeswax

A solid cake of golden beeswax is superior to the apologetic wafer of white near-candlegrease which is sometimes offered; but both will hold the thread from unravelling and will help preserve the stitching. Even soap will fulfil the former task, in default of anything else immediately available when at sea.

Bench hook

Amateur canvas workers who scoff at the bench hook, so beloved by the traditional hand worker, will quickly learn why it is liked once they have tried it; Fig. 1.4. The hook is stuck into the seam and tied away to the right by its lanyard; the left hand can then pull against the hook to steady the work, while the right hand seams the two parts of canvas. The bench hook effectively gives you a third hand.

Fig. 1.4 Bench hook

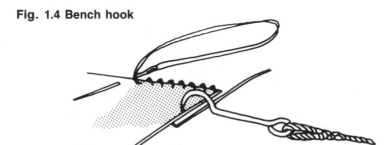

The bench hook provides a third hand to hold the work steady.

Knife

Scissors will cut both thread and cloth, but traditionally the canvas worker uses a knife, held with the blade uppermost when cutting cloth; see that it is razor sharp, always. If you find difficulty in accurate cutting with a knife, however, there is no shame in scissors.

The handle of your knife will make a good rubbing iron, to crease a fold into the cloth before you sew a tabling or hem.

Fids and spikes

A spike of hardwood or metal has been an elementary canvas-working tool for centuries. If it has a sharp point (and is thus made of metal), it is called a spike; if it has a blunt point (of wood) and is larger, it is a fid. A spike is used for separating the strands of a rope before splicing, or for piercing holes in thick canvas for easier sewing; a fid is used for working a cringle or reaming a finished splice. The smaller metal spikes are sometimes known as prickers, and may be adapted from ice-picks or screwdrivers. Large fids are often made of lignum vitae or ebony.

Swedish splicing tool The traditional marlin spike for splicing finds little place in the modern canvas worker's ditty bag. Narrow gauge wires and synthetic ropes are better hand-spliced with a hollow Swedish splicer as illustrated in Fig. 1.5; this penetrates the lay of the cable and allows the passage of the appropriate strand along its groove without having to withdraw the tool first.

Fig. 1.5 Swedish splicing tool

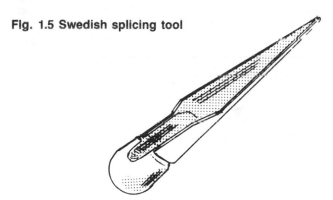

The hollow shape allows one strand of rope to be passed between the other two without removing the spike from the lay.

Serving mallet

The serving mallet will probably be familiar to most of those who venture into canvas work, even if only by sight. It is a specialist tool for the specialist rope or wire worker, and I don't think it has a place in our armoury – certainly not yet awhile. Apart from anything else, we are not training to become even part-time riggers, so the amount of work it will be put to will be minimal. Any serving we propose can be adequately achieved without a special mallet.

Swaging tool

Similarly, I can't see a use for a swaging tool in the sphere of operations we will be undertaking. If much wire splicing is envisaged, then by all means invest in one of the portable swagers which look like a pair of professional wire cutters – but they cost an arm and a leg. They do a good job, depending on the amount of pressure the operator can exert by hand.

Each size of wire needs a specific size of ferrule (copper for stainless, alloy for galvanised wire), and the appropriate die in the tool to fit. Don't try to make the next size up or down fit – *the splice will fail.* Therefore, if you must have a hand swager of your own, make sure that it will accept the correct dies for your rigging needs. The small Nicopress® hand tool which Messrs Sea Sure® of Warsash have kindly allowed me to reproduce from their catalogue at Fig. 1.6, has a twin groove head, covering 2 and 2.5 mm ($^1/_{16}$ and $^3/_{32}$ in) diameter wires; there are also medium and large hand swagers (before you get to bench tools) with three- and four-groove heads, which cover diameters up to 8 mm ($^5/_{16}$ in). But beware, you will be in to three figures for even the small tool, and a good week's wages for the medium size. Not to be undertaken lightly unless you foresee a lot of swaging.

Fig. 1.6 Hand swager

The Nicropress® small hand swaging tool from Sea-Sure's® catalogue covers two sizes of wire.

Cutter, punch and die

We have seen that a spike can be used in order to make a hole in canvas. But it is sometimes better to be more precise, and this is where the cutter and punch come in.

Usually involved in fitting an eyelet of some kind, the complete kit comprises a cutting or wad punch for making a hole slightly smaller than the eye, so that some cloth remains to be gripped by the grommet and its ring; a die on which to place the grommet when it has been fitted to the hole in the cloth; and an inserting punch which, when struck with a hammer, will spread the liner of the turnover over the hole or ring to complete the job; Fig. 1.7. Properly machined tools to sailmaking standards are by no means cheap. There are, however, less expensive products which will do a less expensive job, but which wouldn't stand up to the repeated hammering they would receive from a professional. Hipkiss make them, and they can be found in camping shops and some supermarkets or general stores (Fig. 1.8); just the job for the amateur canvas worker who does not need years of wear from his equipment. The resulting eyelet won't withstand the rough treatment which can be absorbed by a hand-worked eye or one put in by hydraulic press, but it will serve well enough where the stresses aren't going to be excessive.

There is also a special tool shaped like a cross between a pair of pliers and a single-hole paper punch; Fig. 1.9. It is restricted to very small eyelets such as those which might be used for the drawstring of a light carrier bag, and the result is weak.

1.7 Cutter, punch and die

1.8 Amateur's punch and die

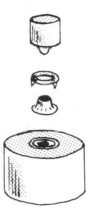

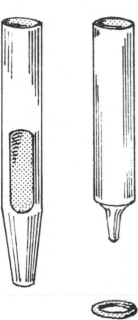

The Hipkiss® set is adequate for the amateur, though even the spur ring shown here gives relatively poor holding.

1.9 Hand punch

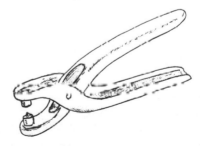

The professional's tools are precision-ground items, and this is reflected in their price.

The hand punch is only suitable for clenching the smallest eyelets.

Heat sealer

Most synthetics can be cut and sealed by the appropriate use of heat; this applies equally to cloth and rope. An electric soldering iron with a wire or blade tip will do the job very well and, for our use, there is no need to invest in an expensive purpose-built tool. You really must have something of the sort if you are going to make anything from scratch, rather than undertake a few minor repairs; make sure that the one you choose has a rating of at least 60 watts, or it will never stay hot enough.

Transfer tape

The introduction of transfer tape (double-sided sticky tape) has made a world of difference, not only to the amateur canvas worker, but to the professional as well; it is widely used in sail lofts. The tape is narrow (1 cm or $\frac{1}{2}$ in) and extremely thin. It comes in reels, and has a waxed backing paper which allows the tape to be unreeled to expose one adhesive surface. This is run the length of the seam and the backing paper is then removed to expose the other side, equally adhesive. If you have any difficulty in starting the backing paper, bend a corner of the tape into a crease, and it should separate easily. The second cloth may then be stuck in position, where it will remain during the sewing process. This ensures an even seam width (if you have put it on carefully), and prevents creep of one cloth on the other, without having to resort to pins, clips or liquid glue. Use of a spray-on silicone release agent, such as BP Adsil D.1® or Ambersil Formula 6®, as a lubricant for the sewing machine needle will minimise any problems which the adhesive might create.

Transfer tape sticks better to some fabrics than others. The rougher the weave the poorer the adhesion but, if carefully handled, it will help in most cases and is a boon to the semi-skilled worker. The sticky side which is first exposed as the tape is unreeled has slightly better adhesion than the one under the backing paper; if you are seaming two cloths of unequal weave, therefore, apply the tape to the poorer surface first.

Workbench

The professional sailmaker will be provided with a bench of convenient height, on which he will keep the tools of his trade: palm, needles, twine, beeswax, knife, rings, etc. The amateur canvas worker should beware of commandeering one of the household chairs or stools. If enough work to warrant setting up in the attic or garage is going to be done, then it is worth saving wear and tear on the furniture (not to say the marital relations) by buying a wooden kitchen stool, cutting its height down, and screwing a special tool tray to its base. The height should ideally be such that the knees are slightly higher than the hips – this will allow the work to be stretched across the lap for convenient sewing.

Figure 1.10 shows the sort of tool tray which I have in mind. There is a rail round the edge to keep everything tidy, and I have carried the tray across to the other side in order to include the traditional holes for keeping spikes and fids handy; you may not need this refinement. A felt pad should stop needles getting lost, and you will doubtless notice the small post with bench hook permanently attached. If nothing else, a tool tray such as this should help you *feel* the part.

1.10 Amateur's work bench

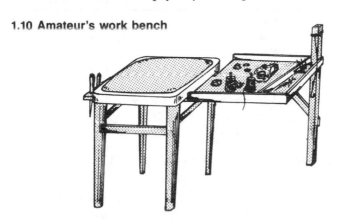

(a)   A tailor-made tray may be attached to a stool or chair.

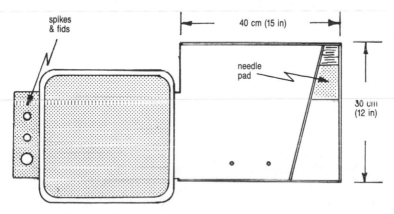

(b)   Plan view: the extension for spikes and fids is by no means essential.

If you are undertaking more than a couple of days' work, it will pay handsomely to organise your tools.

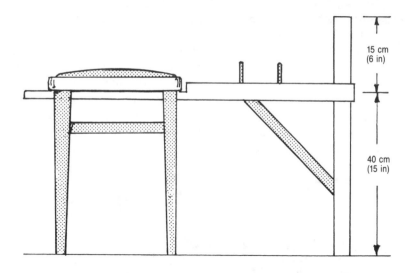

15 cm
(6 in)

40 cm
(15 in)

(c)   Elevation.

The Sewing Machine

It is not likely that an amateur will buy an industrial sewing machine, unless he or she proposes to undertake a major project such as a winter cover for a 35-footer, plus a number of hatch covers and sail coats. So we must look at the domestic or household machine with a view to using it for fairly heavy work.

Requirements

To start with, a certain amount of ruggedness in the machine itself is desirable and, if buying a new one, weight is as good a guide as you will get on what must be no more than a nodding acquaintance. As with many another product, a reasonable standard of engineering is also needed but, as with many another product, price alone will not be a sufficient warranty of quality; you may be paying for unneeded fancy stitch options, and possibly for high distribution or import costs.

Don't ignore the old-fashioned hand-operated machine which has been in the family for ages, and which may or may not have been converted to electric drive. The chances are that it will be a Singer®, and that particular company has always put a lot of quality into its products; the first half of this century saw some beautifully made models which are still giving smooth and trouble-free service; indeed, the Singer 15N is still being produced today. Clean and oil grandma's old trusty, therefore, and possibly fit a new drive belt (or find out about conversion to electricity), and then submit it to the tests suggested below for new machines, before you discard it and rush into a new purchase; it will almost certainly be made to high engineering standards and, if nothing else, will make an excellent work horse for you to learn on. You may end up sticking to it for ever.

All domestic sewing machines work on the same basic principles. The stitch is formed by carefully adjusted interaction of the needle and the shuttle hook on the bobbin assembly. It is not necessary to know the exact mechanics of the operation which forms the stitch – it is sufficient that the needle pushes down through the material, and leaves behind a small loop of thread as it withdraws; the shuttle hook engages this and forms the stitch. Misalignment or poor timing can upset the delicate balance of this precise process, but we shall see shortly the various adjustments which are available to the machinist in order to suit the stitching to the cloth being used.

You may use zig-zag or straight stitch for canvas work, with nearly equal results (there are those who say that a straight stitch is superior); fancy stitch options are not necessary for our use. Your fifty-year-old treadle or hand-operated machine may only have a straight stitch capability, but don't let that put you off, because it will make perfectly good covers.

The amount of canvas which can be worked is sometimes limited by the space under the machine arm. AME is an engineering subsidiary of W G Lucas, the Portsmouth sailmakers, and they can extend the arm clearance of most existing industrial sewing machines.

Tests

Many sewing machine shops and, indeed, department stores, have display machines, with experts to demonstrate and advise. If a chain store has no demonstration machines, its pattern department may be able to help with general advice. Take along a piece of the heaviest canvas you think you will be sewing, with a view to testing it on as many models as you can. Having satisfied yourself that you are looking at a rugged machine which is within your price range, where you will not be paying a lot for gadgets and functions which you do not want (but remember that extra options may be useful for dressmaking later), what tests are there which you can use to assess the quality of the various candidates?

Try turning the mechanism by hand, without any thread (disengage the motor and raise the presser foot first). Note any hard spots in the cycle, and feel for a general smoothness and rhythm. A brand new machine may feel a little tight to start with, but there should be no roughness about its operation.

Next, run it at high speed under power, again without any thread and with the pressure foot raised. Test for the same qualities, and listen for any undue vibration (a screwdriver tip placed at strategic points on the casing, with the handle to your ear, makes an admirable stethoscope, as many car mechanics know). Not until you have compared two or three different makes will you know exactly what it is you are seeking, so you may have to return to your first test machine for a second run; check a very expensive model as well, to establish a yardstick. Machines with the newer rotary shuttle hook are likely to be smoother than those with the older oscillating hook.

Now sew your sample canvas, four or five thicknesses together, with stitching and pressures as advised by the demonstrator; watch the adjustments being made, and note how easy or difficult they are to carry out. Check whether there is any reluctance to form stitches, and whether the work moves easily under the foot. Ask what is the total weight of fabric which the machine will successfully sew (when making reinforced corners, you will have at least three or four thicknesses of heavy cotton or acrylic – more if a seam gets in the way). As a guide, you can look to the following from the different shuttle hook systems.

Type of Shuttle Hook	oz/yd^2(UK)	oz/US	gm/m^2
Oscillating (consistency)	40–60	30–50	1500–2000
Rotary (economy machines)	30–45	25–35	1000–1500
Rotary (expensive machines)	50–70	40–55	1750–2400
Horizontal (less consistency)	30–45	25–35	1000–1500

Table 3. *Total cloth weight capacity of various domestic machine types.*

Some materials (e.g. PVC-coated nylon) tend to stick under the presser foot. This is virtually cured by having either a plastic foot, or else one which is coated with PTFE (non-stick Teflon®); in an emergency, rub the seam with fairly dry bar soap, or do the same to the presser foot (not too liberally, but repeat frequently); baby powder will also help.

Machine needles

Different sewing machines are designed for different needles, and each machine will accept different styles and sizes of needle. J. & P. Coats of Paisley in Scotland (who were kind enough to help with this section) tell me that over 2,000 combinations have been developed. Fortunately, we can cut this number down to manageable proportions.

Style The sharp end of a sewing machine needle can vary according to the material being sewn and the effect which may be desired in the seams. There are three basic classes of point: ball pointed, sharp pointed, and cutting pointed.

Ball-pointed needles   Their rounded point is designed to ease between the loops of knitted fabrics, and they are thus not for the canvas worker. We may dismiss them.

Sharp-pointed needles   These are traditional needles, used since the sewing machine was invented in its present form over a century ago. The style evolved from the domestic hand-sewing needle, and pushes the weave aside with its point as it passes through the fabric. It works well with natural fibres such as cotton and, indeed, with most synthetic fibres, which allow the weave to open slightly to permit passage of the needle, and then to readjust as it is withdrawn. The most common style in this category is the *set-point* needle, which is half way between blunt and sharp, known respectively as *heavy set point* and *plain set point*.

Cutting-pointed needles   As the name implies, these needles have a cutting tip, designed to sever the threads of the weave or to cut a slit in homogeneous fabrics such as vinyl. Film laminates and many polyvinylchloride (PVC) coated cloths do not adjust round a hole made by a needle, and were thus originally liable to puckers from distortion caused in the sewing process. The cutting-pointed needle was designed to overcome this by forming its own slit as it passes. As a spin-off, less needle heat is generated, and this has been found beneficial with some tightly woven made-made cloths (especially when these are covered with a PVC coating), and with leather, neither of which has the same give as a conventional weave. There are several variations of cutting needles, from *spear* to *wedge*, through *triangular* and *diamond*; the *wedge* or *chisel tip* is best for PVC-coated cloth.

Needle size   If the needle is too fine for the thread to run through the eye easily, the thread will be chafed and may break; too fine a needle may also bend, thus affecting formation of the stitch. If the needle is too coarse, on the other hand, stitches may be skipped due to too large a hole in the fabric. The Nm (numero metric) sizing of machine needles relates to the diameter of the blade between the eye and the reinforced shank, expressed in hundredths of a millimetre. Singers have used their own grading since long before metrication (as have other manufacturers) and, because theirs is so well known, its equivalent is shown in Table 4, which gives recommended needle and thread combinations to suit various materials peculiar to our use. General advice is to use as fine a needle as may be compatible with the proposed thread and fabric.

Cloth oz/yd^2					Needle Size	Machine Thread	
Polyester	Nylon	Cotton	Acrylic	PVC	Singer/Nm	Polyester US/Nm	Cotton
2–5	1–3				11/75	V46/50	
		2–6			11/75	V46/50	40
5–8					16/100	V69/30	
			8–10		*14/90	V69/30	
		7–10			18/110	V92/26	24
9–12					19/120	V92/26	
				12–16	**19/120	V92/26	

Table 4. *Recommended machine needle and thread sizes for cover work.*
  * *Acrylic's seemingly fine needle is because the fabric tends to pucker, so as fine a needle as will not break should be used.*
** *Use a wedge- or chisel-pointed needle for PVC.*

Machine thread

For the purpose of working in heavy canvas, the choice of thread to use in the domestic sewing machine lies between polyester and what is called 'mercerised' cotton. There are other threads, notably silk, nylon, soft machine cotton and heavy duty cotton-covered polyester; each has its pro's and con's, but you will be advised to stick with one of the two choices I have suggested, if only for the sake of simplicity. Dyeing tends to make all threads slightly more prone to breakage through being hardened; so use white unless you simply must have colour.

Tension   The stitch link between upper and lower threads should be made between layers if possible; if this cannot always be achieved, it should be hard up against the lower layer. All machines enable tension on either thread to be adjusted. Increasing tension on a thread will draw the link towards the greater tension, more readily than decreasing it on the other side will ease it away from the slackened side. If you buy a new machine, it will have been set up for light materials, and you may need to ease both upper and lower tensions *very slightly* to accommodate thicker fabrics. But don't rush in and alter the careful tuning before you have asked the retailer or service agent if they think that this will be necessary (and take note of the original settings, so that you can always restore them); see Chapter 4; Figs. 4.1 and 4.2.

Polyester thread   Formed of homogeneous extrusions twisted together, most polyester threads are inhibited against the weakening effects of prolonged sunlight, and of many industrial smokes. Polyester machine threads have also usually been treated with silicones to reduce friction, thus helping easy sewing. They do not rot through mildew, and have a certain elasticity (which helps guard against breakage in use) so, in broad terms, they form an almost universal thread for use when machining heavy canvas of most descriptions, and this includes cotton.

Mercerised cotton thread   Named after a nineteenth-century textile manufacturer, mercerising treats the cotton with caustic soda to make it smoother, increase its strength, and help it to take dye more readily. Cotton's advantage over polyester is that it is almost unaffected by ultraviolet rays but, on the other hand, it will rot if it is stored in damp conditions.

Thread size   Machine threads are graded in a multitude of ways relating variously to cotton count, size, weight, ticket numbering, denier or the Tex system, all but one of which have grown up with the industry over the years; the exception is metric numbering (numero metric or Nm). The cotton count (Ne) is widespread but, though it has been adapted to synthetics, it is clearly outdated so we will spend no more time on it. The Tex system is based on the weight in grammes of 1,000 metres of thread, and is conveniently multiplied by 10 in order to express more accurately (as decitex) the small measurements involved. The metric count relates to the number of 1,000 metre hanks per kilogram and, at the sizes we are considering, ranges between Nm 70 (which is light) and Nm 26 (which is coarse). There is a popular American ticket numbering (with a V-prefix) which equates V42 to Nm 70 at the light end, and V92 to Nm 26 at the heavy end of the scale. In fact, you and I may standardise on Nm 30 (the American V69) without running into danger, and this may double as hand twine when working reinforcement patches on very light cotton, polyester or nylon. Table 4 above gives specific recommended thread and needle combinations to suit various fabrics.

Seam ripper

There are special tools such as the Quickunpic®, smaller than a ballpoint pen, available from many stores selling threads and ribbons, which are designed to facilitate unpicking a row of stitching. They work best on zig-zag machine stitching, and are worth having because they are cheap and you won't have lost much if you find later that you can't get on with one of them.

2 The Materials

Evolution of the tools of any trade, of course, will have been influenced over the years by the materials on which they are used, as well as by the applications to which they are put. A review of the principal fabrics and fittings with which we shall be concerned will not only help us select the correct materials, but will also enable us to understand our tools better.

Cloth

Flax

Chronologically speaking, flax comes first in any list of modern sailcloths. It is hard-wearing, soft even when wet, but is heavy, loosely woven, and stretches a lot. In recommending that we may dismiss it for our purposes, I don't want to imply that it finds no place in any cover-maker's inventory, for it is useful for making hard-wearing tilts for industrial use. But the amateur is more likely to be interested in small, easily handled covers, so we may proceed to other fabrics without further ado.

Cotton

Cotton staples are shorter and finer than those of the flax plant. They are also of a woolly and spiral character, which causes resistance between the fibres when they are spun into thread, and enable a uniform and closely woven cloth to be produced.

Reasonably heavy cotton makes an excellent material for covers which need to be waterproof, yet able to breathe (and thus to avoid condensation). Its two drawbacks are a liability to mildew if stored when wet, and a tendency to shrink with the years.

Cotton cloth spans the full weight range from 65–650 gm/m^2 (2–20 oz/yd^2), and a large variety of widths is normally available; Table 5 gives suggested weights for different uses.

Application	gm/m^2	oz/yd^2	oz/US
Light sun awnings, wind scoops	75–150	2–4	1½–3
Hatch covers (proofed)	150–200	4–6	3–5
Small holdalls, bags	150–200	4–6	3–5
Large holdalls	200–275	6–8	5–6
Large covers, tilts (proofed)	300–400	9–12	7–10

Table 5. *Cotton weights for various suggested applications. Equivalents are approximate.*

Polyester

We shall find ourselves increasingly using man-made fibres as we progress. Of these, Terylene® and Dacron® will be prominent. The advantages of polyester are that it is easy to work, and stable in performance; the edges may be heat sealed to prevent fraying; and there is little distortion, even on the bias, under the loadings we are considering. Polyester's disadvantages are that it is not waterproof unless it is impregnated by resins or other chemicals (which don't always adhere to the weave too well); it suffers from degradation if exposed to the ultraviolet rays of sunlight for prolonged periods (this can be inhibited to a certain extent during the weaving and finishing process, but it is not 100%). It does not dye readily, so that economics dictate that colours are restricted to fairly light cloths (under 150 gm/m^2 or 5 oz/yd^2). Table 6 gives some suggested polyester cloth weights.

Application	gm/m^2	oz/yd^2	oz/US
Small covers	100–150	3–4	2–3
Lee cloths	175	5	4
Fender covers	175–250	5–7	4–6

Table 6. *Polyester weights for various suggested applications. Equivalents are approximate only.*

Nylon

Nylon is not the kind of material we normally associate with covers, but it finds a place in this book largely because I shall be recommending it later for the wind scoop and for the Spi Strangler; it is also sometimes used for sailbags. It is light, and thus not waterproof, will chafe easily, and is weakened by ultraviolet rays. Its advantages are that it is easily worked, is not weakened by mildew (though it will discolour from mildew picked up by dirt particles adhering to the weave), and it stows in a small space; it also comes in a wide variety of colours if desired.

Nylon often forms the base for the PVC-coated fabrics which are so suitable for sail coats, hatch covers and the like (not that you would notice). The following Table 7 gives some suggested weights.

Application	gm/m^2	oz/yd^2	oz/US
Spi Strangler	50	1½	1
Wind scoops/wind breaks	75–100	2–3	1½–2
Sailbags	150–200	4–6	3–5

Table 7. *Nylon weights for various suggested applications. Equivalents are approximate only.*

Film laminates

Film laminates were developed to improve sail shape through reduced distortion. They rule themselves out as cover materials through half a dozen reasons:

(a) They are very expensive;
(b) They are difficult to work;
(c) They chafe badly;
(d) They are subject to UV degradation;
(e) They can suffer from delamination;
(f) They are difficult and expensive to repair

Polyethelene

Polyethelene is a light thermoplastic film which, when used as a cheap fabric in its own right (rather than as a laminated backing for a fine woven cloth), is normally bolstered by a light mesh moulded into the film. Because it is a film, it does not close round any hole which is made in it, and stitch holes are liable to become enlarged under load if the built-in mesh is not strong enough.

It is completely waterproof (except for seams, unless they are specially treated with Duroseam®, Seamkote® or the like), and does not distort under the normal loads we are considering; it will withstand a surprising amount of rough use, though it will wear badly if subjected to prolonged chafe. It does, however, suffer chemical degradation from ultraviolet rays; once it starts to decay, it deteriorates rapidly.

A cheap and cheerful fabric, therefore, which is usually associated with coarsely made products, which become 'throw-away' items when they start to fail.

Use Polyethelene forms an ideal material for supermarket trolley bags, garden weed sheets or general tidy bags.

Coated cloths

As I have already hinted, fabrics which have been coated in one way or another are going to figure largely in these pages. This is particularly true where there is a need for waterproof covers. Cloth which in itself is permeable can be coated with polyvinylchloride (PVC) or one of the spray-on silicones, to render it waterproof. This not only proofs the fabric, but gives it body.

The two principal candidates for our attention are the treated acrylics and PVC-coated nylon or polyester. There is virtually nothing to beat these in my opinion, when it comes to marine cover work.

Acrylic This is a cloth of some 250–350 gm/m^2 (6–8 oz/US or 8–10 oz/yd^2) in its marine application, which has usually been subjected to a chemical proofing such as Scotchgard® when used for boat covers. The fabric has plenty of body, with a matt finish and a soft handle; as such it doesn't show creases easily and it hangs well. It will 'breathe' very slightly, and its rich feel and appearance make it popular for hatch covers, sail coats, etc. Its main drawback is the tendency of any soft cloth to pucker slightly under the sewing machine, so that as small a needle as will not regularly break is advised. It is also rather less chafe- and tear-resistant than most PVC-coated fabrics.

PVC-coated canvas There is a wide range of cloths (usually nylon or polyester based) which have been coated with polyvinylchloride, and their application is equally wide. Most PVC materials for use as spray dodgers or covers on yachts fall within a weight range of 400–550 gm/m^2 (10–13 oz/US or 12–16 oz/yd^2), when the proofing has been taken into consideration. Several widths are available so if you need something extra broad to avoid an awkward seam (see *Sail Covers* in Chapter 7), it is worth shopping around (a 2.5 m or 8 ft wide cloth is available in the UK in 18 oz/yd^2). PVC cloth is so completely waterproof that condensation occurs inside covers unless provision is made for air circulation. The material is best machined with a chisel-pointed needle, which will cut the coating to allow easy passage of the thread; don't forget my remarks in Chapter 1 about the use of PTFE, bar soap or even baby powder to prevent the material sticking under the machine foot.

Attachments

Eyes and eyelets

You could be forgiven for asking what the difference is between eyes and eyelets. The answer is that there is very little, except that I have taken eyes to be larger than eyelets so, as far as this book is concerned, an eye is a hand-worked ring sewn into the canvas with needle and palm, and with a protecting liner or turnover hammered into it to stop the stitching from fraying; an eyelet is punched into the canvas and clenched directly onto the cloth (as such it is weaker than an eye).

The professional may well use a hydraulic press to fit an eye, and the result can be even stronger than a hand sewn ring. But the machine costs thousands, so we are restricted to the punch and die described in Chapter 1.

Punched eyelet The various parts of a punched eyelet are shown in Fig. 2.1. It will be seen that a simple turnover may be used on its own (a), with upstanding thimble piece (funnel) to grip the cloth rather weakly when it is spread. A better job is made if the turnover is spread over a superimposed plain ring as a backing plate (b). An even better grip is obtained if a spur or toothed ring (which will also grip the cloth in its own right) is used (c).

Fig. 2.1 Eyelets

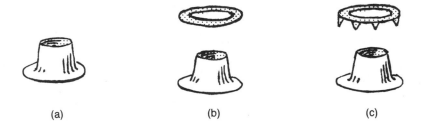

(a) (b) (c)

(a) Simple eyelet with turnover to grip the cloth.
(b) Eyelet with plain, flat ring as backing plate.
(c) Eyelet with spur or toothed ring.

Hand-sewn eye If fairly heavy loadings are expected, as from a tarpaulin tie, tent guy, or awning lashing, a hand-sewn eye should be used. Figure 2.2(a) shows the component parts, and these need to be assembled with the aid of the appropriate punch and die (Fig. 1.7), after the ring has been hand sewn. Eyes for use in a marine atmosphere must be made of bronze or they will corrode; the join should be welded or brazed, not left open. Because the tools to spread the turnover liner are expensive (for each set you could comfortably dine out with your spouse, or with somebody else's for that matter), it is a good idea to fix on not more than two sizes of eye, and stick to those – one if you can manage it. It is worth asking your sailmaker if he has a worn set which he will sell you cheaply – he can't afford to fiddle with a blunt or chipped cutter, or accept a bent turnover, whereas you and I may settle for some slight inconvenience if it reduces the price dramatically.

Fig. 2.2 Eyes

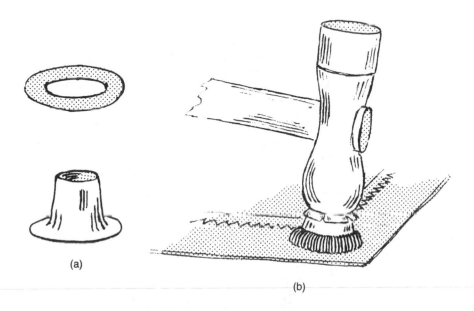

(a)

(b)

An eye gets its strength from the solid ring which is sewn to the canvas itself.
(a)   The ring (which should have a welded or brazed joint), with its turnover for protecting the stitching.
(b)   The turnover may be spread over the stitching and ring by means of a punch and die (Fig. 1.7) or, if that is not available, by careful hammering (amateur punch sets are not always suitable).

There is an alternative to buying a costly punch and die set. The turnover can be carefully started by resting the ball-pein end of an engineer's hammer on top of it, and then hitting it with another hammer until the turnover starts to splay out; finish the job by direct hammering; Fig. 2.2(b). Practise first on a piece of scrap canvas, if you don't want to see the ruin of hours of careful sewing, through overhitting and cutting the cloth. The Hipkiss amateur sets shown in Fig. 1.8 are usually not man enough for a large eye. The principles of sewing are illustrated in Fig. 2.3 and explained in detail in the next chapter.

Fig. 2.3 Hand-sewn eye

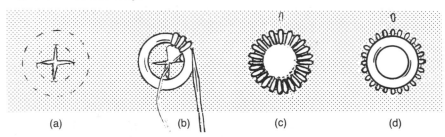

(a)   (b)   (c)   (d)

A hand-sewn eye provides great strength, as can be seen from the way it becomes an integral part of the canvas, gripping the edges of the cruciform hole. The turnover protects the stitching from chafe, and does not contribute to strength. See Fig. 3.10 for details.

D-rings   Yet another alternative to the punch and die is to fit a plain or D-shaped ring on a webbing tab sewn to the uncut cloth; Fig. 2.4. It should be bronze or stainless steel for marine use, and should be a continuous ring with a welded or brazed joint if there is any danger of it buckling under load.

Fig. 2.4 Tab rings

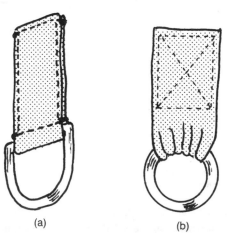

(a)   (b)

Another form of strong eye is provided by tab rings.
(a)   A D-ring gives the firmest fit. Hand stitching is taken round the edge of the tab, and each corner has been given extra round stitches as reinforcement.
(b)   A round ring may have to be used, but make sure that its joint is welded or brazed (as you should for the D-ring). The machine stitching shown here has been run across the diagonal for security; again, the corners may be reinforced with a few hand stitches.

Fasteners

Lashings which are tied via a series of eyelets or loops are tedious to use, and there are various other methods of fastening canvas either to itself or to a rigid structure. The accompanying drawings show some of the hardware available; most of them come in nickle-plated brass (though you may have to order it specially). Their application is discussed in the next chapter.

Where a fastener is clenched to canvas by means of a backing plate or specialist washer, a special tool is often sold to cut the holes in the correct places (and don't run away with the idea that one cutter will deal with every clinch plate – the different fasteners have their teeth differently spaced). The joy of not being a professional is that you may spend a little more time on the job, so that you will not need to buy those special tools; with patience, a sharp knife and a pair of pliers will do the job.

Press-stud fastener   The male stud of what is sometimes known as the durable dot, or snap fastener, may screw to a rigid structure with a self-tapping or a wood screw as in Fig. 2.5(a); it is also available with a machine-screw ending. For fitting to canvas, it may be clenched by what is called in the catalogue an eyelet (b). The female socket is normally always clenched to the canvas by means of a button (c). These press studs may come undone fairly easily if not securely fastened.

Fig. 2.5 Press-stud fastener

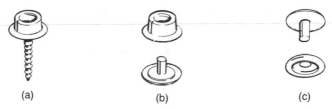

(a)   (b)   (c)

The press stud is popular because it offers little in the way of obstructions to catch or be caught.
(a)   The male stud may be screwed to the superstructure. Machine screw and self-tapping screw fittings are also obtainable.
(b)   The stud may need to be clenched to canvas for cloth-to-cloth fitting.
(c)   The female socket is always clenched to canvas against a clinch plate.

Lift-the-dot-fastener   Here again the male stud may either screw to a rigid structure as in Fig. 2.6(a), or be attached to canvas by means of a clinch plate or washer (b). The female socket is attached to the canvas by means of a clinch plate (c); it incorporates a spring, so beware of corrosion. The male stud sticks up sharply, ready to catch on small lines or on clothing; it is vulnerable to damage, and will not fasten if it is bent.

Turnbutton fastener This is known in the USA as the common sense fastener, and is the most secure of the three we have so far looked at, but its button is more of an obstruction than even the lift-the-dot stud. The male part, with the turning button, may either be attached to a rigid structure by two wood screws as in Fig. 2.7(a), or by a machine screw fitting, or else clenched to canvas by prongs to a clinch plate (b). The female eyelet is clenched to a washer (c). In some makes, the original metal spring incorporated in the male half has now been replaced by a corrosion-free plastic cushion which does the same job, so it is worth checking on this.

Fig. 2.6 Lift-the-dot fastener

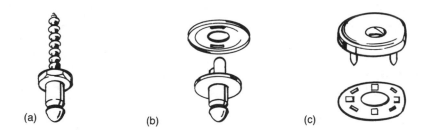

(a) (b) (c)

This provides a secure fastening, but the stud is somewhat vulnerable to knocks.
(a)   The male stud may be screwed to the superstructure.
(b)   The stud may alternatively be clenched to cloth.
(c)   The female socket is clenched to canvas against a clinch plate.

Fig. 2.7 Turnbutton or common sense fastener

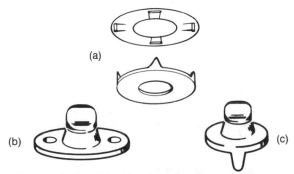

(a)

(b)   (c)

The ultimate in security is offered by the turnbutton, but here again the button is vulnerable to knocks.
(a)   The female socket and clinch plate.
(b)   The male turnbutton may be screwed to the superstructure.
(c)   The turnbutton may be clenched to canvas for cloth-to-cloth fastening.

Pull-knob fastener This may be known as the Tenax® car button, and both parts are screwed onto the canvas by locking nuts clamping onto spurs; Fig. 2.8. A sophisticated fastening (with attendant price) which holds cloth-to-cloth very well, but with a spring which may be vulnerable to a marine atmosphere, and a knob on one side and a peg on the other, both of which can be damaged more easily than a less obtrusive flat button.

Hooks and eyes There is a wide variety of hooks and eyes on the market. To avoid corrosion, the mariner will want to stick to bronze, stainless steel or plastic, unless the canvas work in question will have a short life, when it is pointless spending extra money on durable hooks which will outlast the cover or awning. Explain your needs to your sailmaker or camping shop, and ask them to show you a few examples; there are some very ingenious products about, including tape with small mating hooks and eyes already attached.

Fig. 2.8 Pull-knob fastener

| (a) | (b) | (c) | (d) |

This fastener is often used by the motor trade for open car covers.
(a) and (b)   The female knob with its screwed backing nut.
(c) and (d)   The male peg with spur tooth backing nut.

Zip fasteners It is important for the yachtsman to use zippers whose teeth are made of plastic (Delrin® is good), because metal ones quickly corrode in salt air. The slider will almost certainly be metal, because its function requires it to be too thin for plastic to survive, so make sure that this part is well enamelled; it pays to fit an extra slider where a lot of use is expected, so that you have a reserve in the event of failure, without having to dismantle the whole thing. The choice then lies between the conventional robust chain zip with individual teeth, or the more flexible coil type with continuous synthetic strand (Optilon® is good).

Velcro® Velcro is included here because it does exactly the same job as the metal fasteners just described. Adhesion is not quite so secure (it is better in shear than in peel), but there is not quite the need for such precision in siting the two parts, it is corrosion-free, and it is simplicity itself in operation. It is easy to sew on, and can be as easily shifted if the fit proves inexact.

Rope and cord

There are some half a dozen common types of rope, each very different from the next, but we only need consider two of them: three-strand laid polyester and three-strand laid polypropylene. We can forget all forms of natural fibre rope (manila, cotton, hemp, sisal, etc), because it stretches badly under load and also shrinks and rots with time; we may similarly ignore all braided constructions, because they are expensive and we don't need to pay the premium for soft handling; nylon (too elastic and slippery) and polyethylene (weaker than polyester) can go the same way.

Cord is really small diameter rope. In this book I take it to be less than 3–4 mm diameter or $1/2$ in circumference. A useful rule of thumb is that 1 mm diameter equals $1/8$ in circ. exactly, i.e. 8 mm dia. = 1 in circ.; 11 mm dia. = $1^3/8$ in circ., and so on.

Three-strand laid polyester The canvas worker won't have a big requirement for rope. He or she may need small quantities of lashings for awnings or tilts, and they shouldn't stretch too much in use, or shrink when wet. Pre-stretched 3-strand laid polyester (Terylene or Dacron) is the answer to almost all his needs, and it has the extra advantage that it won't rot and is easy to work (it can be heat sealed to prevent it fraying, and is easy to splice with a Swedish splicing tool – but give it four tucks per strand instead of the more usual three, because it is slightly more slippery than natural fibre rope).

Three-strand laid polypropylene The polyester rope described above could really stand by itself as the canvas worker's all-purpose cordage, but polypropylene gets a mention purely because it floats. It has inferior wearing qualities to polyester (it is actually stronger wet than dry) but, if there is a requirement for a floating rope (dinghy painters won't wrap around propellers; water skiers like a floating tow-rope; lifelines on a bathing beach are better if they float), then polypropylene is the answer. It splices almost too easily (it can pull loose), so give it at least five tucks per strand, and whip the end result.

Cord Amost any kind of cord will do for light lashings on covers, etc. Polyester is best for the same reasons as for rope, and nylon is worst because it is so slippery that it is hard to tie it securely. As there is little call for splicing in these small sizes, braided cord is just as good as three-strand laid, if not better; there is little price difference in these sizes. Always heat seal the ends.

Wire

The canvas worker will have even less call for wire than for rope. If you do need to use it, get hold of a good book on wire splicing, which also covers the use of swaging tools and bulldog grips. If it is needed, make sure that you get stainless steel (but be aware that PVC-covered stainless steel can suffer deterioration due to oxygen starvation through what is known as shielding corrosion); standing rigging needs stiff wire of the 1×19 variety, while running rigging needs the flexibility of a 7×7 construction or something similar. Splicing wire is outside the scope of this book, but I must not shirk recommending the use of Talurit® or Nicopress swaging – it is worth paying a bit to get a rigger to do it for you if peace of mind and safety depend on the result, but see Fig. 1.6 in the previous chapter.

Shock cord
Shock cord is a fancy name for elastic, which finds a use for quick fastening purposes. 5–6 mm dia. (³/₄ in circ.) is as small as you should go for cover fastenings, or it will perish too quickly; 8 mm dia. is a stout size.

Webbing and tape
As with eyes and eyelets, there is very little difference between webbing and tape. I have taken it to be one of width and fineness of weave; webbing is coarse and wide (over 4 cm or 1½ in) and thus very strong, while tape is fine and narrow (under 5 cm or 2 in).

Use The canvas worker uses tape for reinforcing where necessary (windbreak tablings, awning ridges or sea anchor rims), and webbing for making an item in itself (cook's harness or bo'sun's chair).

Window material
Window material is clear PVC, and for durability you need at least 0.4 mm if not 0.5 mm thickness (16 or 19 gauge). Bainbridge Aquabatten call their product Plastipane®; there are others called Velbex® and Glasclear®. When buying, check on flexibility as well as durability.

All window material will sew easily by machine but, once a tear has started, it will tend to run, so that care not to give it sharp bends in use is an obvious requirement; repair tape sticks to it well. The material eventually degrades with weathering, but can be replaced if the cloth around it has not done the same.

Adhesive repair tape
Repair tape came into being because yacht racing crews demanded a quick and efficient method of temporarily patching torn spinnakers. An adhesive backing was given to a 5 cm (2 in) wide strip of nylon, and it proved an

instant success. Light nylon of 50 gm/m^2 (1½ oz) is still the most commonly available, but it *can* be found in heavier polyester. It sticks well to most smooth dry surfaces, provided they are clean (it sticks best of all to film, and worst to rough fabrics such as cotton or acrylic). It will normally last a season, particularly if helped out with a few hand stitches, or is pressed on with a hot iron.

Its use for the canvas worker is to hold together a tear so that a proper patch may be applied, or to give some body to a machine darn (Fig. 5.3); it may even be used as a repair in its own right in an emergency – when it will probably still be there long after you have forgotten how the tear was caused.

3 Hand Sewing

Canvas working requires hand work and machine sewing in about equal proportions, so you might as well get used to the idea right away. Pick up that new palm we discussed in Chapter 1, and start to mould it to the shape of your hand. Don't be put off by tales of long apprenticeships for sailmaking – rudimentary hand sewing to satisfy our requirements is not difficult to learn.

Almost all your hand sewing will be done with doubled twine which, if you are embarking on more than a single small job and have taken my advice, will be taken from a cop of the stuff. Unreel about 1½ m (5 ft), any more will make the sewing process unwieldy, any less will mean frequent joins. If it is not prewaxed, wax the tip of one end and thread it through the chosen needle; equalise the two parts and allow any twists to unravel as they hang down. Draw the doubled twine two or three times across your beeswax block, so that the two parts adhere nicely to each other; tie the two ends together in a knot. Professional sailmakers more often leave the starting end unknotted under the first two or three stitches, but you are not aiming to become a full-time sailmaker; it is simplest to tie a figure-of-eight knot with both hands.

Basic stitch

The standard round stitch involves an over-and-over process, and we shall see as we go along that this forms the basis of many another type of hand sewing: seaming, tabling, working an eye, and roping; Fig. 3.1(a). The other basic stitch is one which passes back and forth from one side to the other of the work, in a form of tacking stitch; Fig. 3.1(b). To effect the latter, you have to be able to get at both sides of the job, often with a friend on the other side to speed things up.

Stick a piece of surgical plaster or tape over the back of your thumb, where the sewing palm presses just above the knuckle. Just like any other piece of nautical kit which is subjected to chafe, your skin will rub raw

Fig. 3.1 Basic stitches (hand)

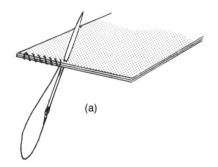

(a) The round hand stitch, using an over-and-over process, and on which many other stitches are based.

(b) The tacking stitch where the needle is passed back and forth through the work.

unless fitted with a protection of some sort – until it hardens, that is. Hold the needle between thumb and forefinger, with its eye resting against the needle plate, then insert the point into the cloth; Fig. 3.2(a). Release your hold and use the palm to push the needle through the fabric (b). As it emerges from the other side, grasp it with thumb and forefinger again to help it out, and then pull the thread through (c). If you find that you regularly have to use pliers to pull the needle through, you are probably using too small a needle. The process should become one continuous movement, and a seasoned canvas worker's hand can literally become a blur when he is round stitching.

Fig. 3.2 Using the palm

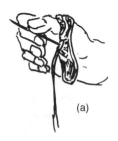

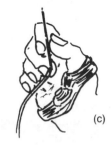

Hold the needle between the thumb and first finger, with the eye against the needle plate, as in (a). Insert the needle in the canvas, release your hold and push it throught with the plate, as in (b). Pick up the needle on the other side of the work, pull in through, and repeat the process (c).

Fig. 3.3 The canvas worker on his bench

This worker is using the home-made work tray of Fig. 1.10, with the bench hook of Fig. 1.4 tied away to the post on his right, as he sews a seam while wearing his apron from Fig. 1.1, using the flat seaming stitch of Fig. 3.5 (quite the little hero).

Hand seaming

There are many ways to join two pieces of canvas together. Most of these involve the sewing machine, as we shall see later, but it can happen that a suitable one is not available, or that the work cannot be properly presented to the machine, so that hand sewing has to be adopted. The kind of seam to be used will depend on the strength needed, whether the work can or cannot be approached from both sides, and whether the result must be waterproof.

The most convenient way for many right-handed workers is to progress from right to left along the work. Start by taking a couple of round stitches at the edge as an anchor, and then proceed to push the needle into the canvas from the far side with the point facing towards your left shoulder; Fig. 3.3. It sounds complicated until it is tried. Aim to sew 2 stitches per centimetre (5–6 per inch); any fewer looks untidy because the spacing is too wide, any more will be too close for convenience. Pull the work to one side with the left hand, against the strain of a bench hook tied off to the right to steady it.

Round seam   If a single line of stitching is considered strong enough, and waterproofing is not a major factor, the round seam of Fig. 3.4 may be used. A raw finish is left on one side, but this is acceptable where the work is tackled from the inside, and then reversed right side out at the finish to leave the raw seam hidden. The round seam is an occasion when sewing may be more convenient from left to right; the stitches should not be pulled too tight or the seam will not open the right way out, flat without wrinkles. This kind of seam is often used at the bottom of a kitbag or ditty bag.

Fig. 3.4 Round seam (hand)

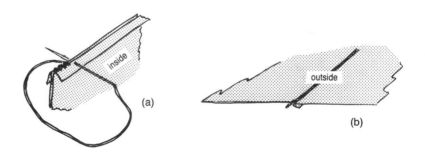

This seam is worked from the inside (a), using the round stitch of Fig. 3.1. Do not pull it too tight, or the results will not open nice and flat as in (b).

Flat seam   Greater strength and reasonable proofing are offered by the flat seam, which is the way sails were made by hand in the days of King Cotton. It has two rows of stitching and an uncomplicated process, particularly if two selvedges are involved or if the edges can be heat sealed, so that they do not have to be tucked under to prevent fraying. Overlap depends on circumstance: 1–3 cm (³⁄₈–1¹⁄₄ in) is usually enough, and this should be marked at intervals along the seam or, better still, the two cloths should be joined with transfer tape (double-sided sticky tape) before starting. Begin at the right with a couple of anchor or holding stitches, and work your way to the left as shown in Fig. 3.5(a). When the first edge is complete, turn it all over so that the cloth nearer you is again on top, and repeat the process; Fig. 3.5(b).

Fig. 3.5 Flat seam (hand)

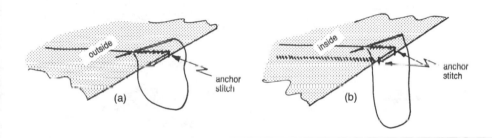

A simple overlap (with the nearer cloth on top) is sewn along its far edge with the flat seaming stitch (a). Work from right to left, with the needle being pushed into the canvas pointing back towards your left shoulder. The work is then turned over and the process repeated down the other edge (b). Note the anchor stitches at the start of each row. Finish in the same manner.

Flat felled seam   If, however, a fully waterproof strong join is required, the flat felled seam is as good as any. To 'fell' is to fold the edges of a seam under and sew them flat – in this case they are interleaved as well, and Fig. 3.6 shows the principle. The lower cloth is allowed to protrude from the upper cloth by 2–3 cm (³⁄₄–1¹⁄₄ in) or so, as in (a). This overlap is then folded over the upper edge and fastened with transfer tape before being anchored and then sewn down from right to left (b). When the first row of stitching is complete, the upper cloth is folded over the seam just produced and again fastened with transfer tape (c). The work is turned back and a second row of stitching is made down the other edge of the seam (d).

Fig. 3.6 Flat felled seam (hand)

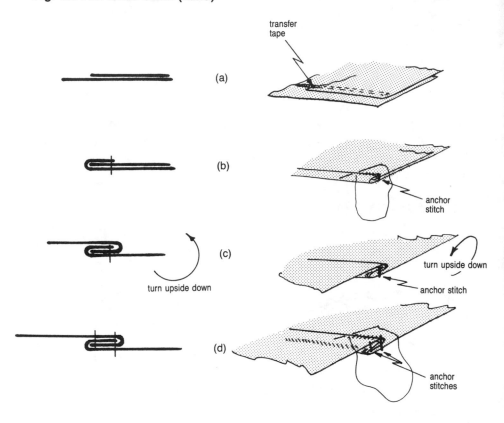

This is the seam to use if waterproofing is important. Lay one panel on top of the other, overlapping slightly, and using transfer tape to hold the two together (a). Then fold the overlap round the end of the upper panel, rub the crease, anchor the corner and sew along the seam (b) with the flat seaming stitch of Fig. 3.5. Now fold the bottom cloth over the finished row of stitching and turn the work upside down (c). Sew the second edge as the first (d).

Tabling

Hems are called tablings in sailmaking, and I beg indulgence to continue the custom of a lifetime here. Where an edge has to be turned in, either to add strengh (for possible acceptance of eyelets), or else to prevent fraying, the tabling process takes place.

Turn the edge of the canvas over by something between 2–5 cm ($^3/_4$–2 in) depending on circumstances (weight of canvas, size of job, presence of a drawstring or eyelets, etc). You will not need double-sided sticky tape to hold it in place, for you should be able to fix a crease in most cloths by rubbing it with the back of your knife handle, or the closed blades of your scissors; Fig. 3.7. A few pencil marks should suffice to ensure a good line.

Place the job across your knees with the turned flap of the tabling on top and pointing away from you. Sew from right to left with the basic round stitch which we used on the edge of the flat seam – starting with one or two anchor stitches to make a firm base.

Fig. 3.7 Simple tabling (hand)

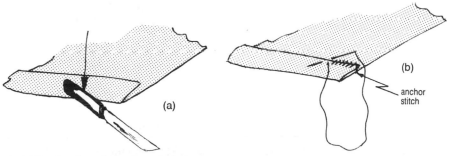

Fold the heat sealed edge of cloth over, and crease it with a rubbing iron of some sort, as in (a). Anchor the corner and sew as in (b) with the flat seaming stitch of Fig. 3.5.

Herringbone stitch

The other name for this stitch is the sailmaker's darn. It is used for drawing the two edges of a tear together, and therefore should not be pulled more than just even at each stitch or the job will pucker up. It can also be used for putting body into a piece of canvas which is chafed but not yet holed.

Sailmaker's herringbone The sailmaker's herringbone stitch is slightly different from that of the dressmaker. Figure 3.8 shows the method of the sail loft and, like round seaming, it is usually worked from left to right. In his books on sails and canvas (referenced at the end), Percy Blandford recommends making alternate stitches longer in order to spread the strain over different parts of the weave. I see no reason to object to this advice, though I feel that it tends to destroy the neat effect when done by the amateur.

Dressmaker's herringbone The dressmaker's version of the same stitch is shown in Fig. 3.9. Its principal disadvantage for our application is that it makes double the number of holes in the canvas, just when we are trying to put strength back into it (in fairness to dressmakers, they have smaller needles than ours and they use the stitch for other purposes).

Fig. 3.8 Herringbone stitch (sailmaker's)

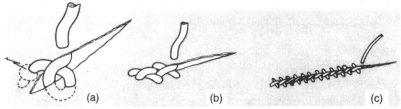

(a) (b) (c)

Knot the end and bring the needle up behind the cross thread (a). Don't pull the stitch too tight or you will crease the result. Make sure you sew into sound canvas each time.

Fig. 3.9 Herringbone stitch (dressmaker's)

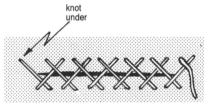

knot
under

This is unnecessarily complicated for the sailmaker, and makes too many holes. I only show it so that you shall recognise and avoid it.

Hand-sewn eye

Site the bronze ring on the canvas, and draw circles round the inside and outside circumferences. You may then either punch a hole *very much smaller* than the inside circle, or else use a knife to make cruciform cuts inside the inner circle; Fig. 3.10(a). This ensures that there is plenty of canvas to sew to the ring, so that it can grip the cloth and make a strong job of it.

Place the ring on the cut and sew down through the cloth on the outside circle, usually starting on the side furthest away from you. A stopper knot will hold the thread, but this is one of the occasions when even the amateur may want to tuck the starting end under the first three or four stitches – there are so many of them, so closely spaced, that holding power is not in doubt. Bring the needle up through the ring and repeat the process round the circumference as in (b), taking care to see that the two parts of twine are not twisted, and that they lie evenly side by side right next to the previous stitch (this is purely for appearance, but few of us would want to spoil what even the veriest tyro can turn into a good-looking job). As with the herringbone, Percy Blandford has suggested that every other stitch should be taken further away from the ring, with the alternate ones kept close to it. He maintains that this is both attractive and, because a close row of stitch holes is avoided, also stronger. This is one of the few points on canvas work where I take issue with Percy. This star effect requires accurate hand sewing if it is not to look disorganised rather than decorative, and the average amateur might find it hard to attain the required precision. Secondly, the 'cornflake packet effect' (where the canvas is liable to tear along the dotted line) is not at all likely, unless you are unwise enough to be working in film laminates or clear PVC; in any event, such staggering would make little difference one way or the other.

Continue sewing round until the ring is fully enclosed (c). The use of the turnover now becomes obvious; without it the stitching would be chafed through by a shackle, cord, tent pole, or what ever is placed through the eye. Put the turnover on the special recess in the die, with the sewn ring on top of it so that the collar of the turnover's funnel protrudes through the top. The point of the punch is placed in the collar and tapped to spread it over the stitching. When it has started nicely, hammer harder to finish the job; Fig. 3.10(d). Note that the strength of this eye does not depend on the grip of the turnover, which need be no more than a firm fit.

Fig. 3.10 Hand-sewn eye

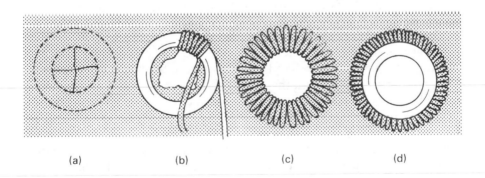

(a) (b) (c) (d)

This is the full procedure for the technique illustrated in Fig. 2.3.

(a)   Cut a cruciform slit, leaving flaps to be sewn in. Mark inside and outside circumferences of the ring.

(b)   Place the ring on the marking and, usually starting on the side away from you, pass the needle down through the outer circumference and up through the middle. Some say that it helps to spread the load if alternate stitches are taken further away from the ring, but I suspect that it is a misguided attempt to make the result look fancier (which will probably have the opposite effect for the amateur); the professional doesn't do it.

(c)   Continue until the ring is fully sewn. You will do more for neatness if you flatten each doubled thread carefully in alignment.

(d)   Protect with a turnover. Spread it firmly but not harshly for, unlike the punched eyelet, strength comes not from the turnover but from the sewn ring.

Punched eyelet

Fitting a punched eyelet is more or less the same as a sewn eye, with the important exceptions that the hand-worked ring is omitted, and the eyelet derives its strengh only from metal gripping cloth.

See Chapter 2 for a description of the different eyelets which are available. Strength depends on the washer or grommet ring: absence of any ring gives a simple spread to the turnover, with poor holding power; Fig. 2.1(a). A simple washer or flat ring improves the grip by providing a form of backing plate; Fig. 2.1(b). A flat ring with spur teeth makes sure that the cloth is gripped both sides (from some sources you can get 'toothed' rings which have straight spikes, or 'spur' rings which have rolled edges to give a slightly better grip); Fig. 2.1(c).

It will be seen that, unlike the sewn ring of a hand-worked eye, a punched eyelet is not physically attached to the cloth. It depends, for any strength it may have, entirely on gripping canvas between two parts of a correctly pressed fitting. It is thus crucial that too much cloth should not be cut away when making the hole for it. This should be done either with a spike (for small eyelets), or by means of two knife cuts in the form of a cross (for bigger ones). When making a tabling which you know is going to receive eyelets, it is advisable to tuck the edge right under to form three layers of cloth for the spur rings to grip; see Fig. 4.6(c).

The turnover or liner is placed on the special metal block, as for a hand-sewn eye, and the hole in the canvas is forced down over the collar. The flat ring or washer is then fitted over the part of the collar which should now be protruding through the canvas. The pointed end of the punch is placed in the middle of the assembly, so that hammering will squeeze the two parts firmly together; Fig. 1.8. Try one or two on scrap canvas first, because too little hammering will leave the parts not gripping the cloth properly; too much may split the turnover or cut the cloth – perhaps both.

If you don't have the correct punch and die, use a lead block as a die, and a blunt spike or centre-punch to start spreading the turnover; finish the job by tapping carefully direct on the eyelet, preferably with the round end of a ball-pein engineer's hammer; see Fig. 2.3.

Very small eyelets, applied by means of a special tool shaped like a cross between a paper punch and a pair of pliers (Fig. 1.9), find a use for filing papers but have pretty poor holding power in canvas.

Roping

There will not often be a need to fit a rope along the edge of a cover or awning, and this is an activity more suited to the sailmaker than the canvas worker. But a heavy duty tarpaulin may benefit from having its corners roped, a sea anchor will need strength round its edges, and a cockpit awning might require supporting with a rope along its spine fore and aft.

A roping needle will be larger than the one you use for seaming or patching the same cloth, and it is a good idea to blunt the point. This stops it entering the strands of the rope too readily, rather than passing between the lay. If you are going to hand sew more than half a dozen stitches, or to turn a corner, you will be advised to straighten the rope so that it is without kinks, then run a pencil down its full length; this will reveal if it is twisting during the sewing process, which would crease the finished job. In addition, offer the rope to the canvas and place match marks across them both at intervals of 20–30 cm (8–12 in); this will show whether the rope starts to follow its usual practice and finish before the canvas runs out, through what is known as 'creep' (or the vanishing rope trick).

Place the edge of the canvas facing you across your knees, and put the left end of the rope just under it. Turn the work up through 90 degrees and, if you have a longish run to sew, tie a bench hook away to your right. Knot the end of your twine and insert the needle under one strand of rope and then through the edge of the canvas, pull the stitch tight and bring the needle back over the work towards you, to pass it under the next strand in what is virtually the basic round stitch; Fig. 3.11. Try not to sew through the strands rather than between them, or you may cause wrinkles (but it's not very serious); pull each stitch with the same tension, for the same reason.

Fig. 3.11 Hand roping

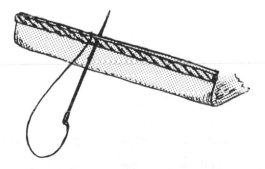

Place the rope under the edge to be sewn, and turn both canvas and rope up through 90 degrees. Pass a large (no. 12 or 13) needle with a dulled point between the lay of the rope and through the canvas. Bring the needle back over the top and repeat the process. You will find that you get through rope more quickly than canvas, and will need to make a conscious effort to keep the two in step; put on match marks before you start, so that the two are sewn at the same rate.

Watch the pencil line you drew along the length of the rope to see that it doesn't twist, and keep an eye on creep. Match marks on the rope will tend to appear before those on the canvas, and you will need to make a conscious effort to take in more cloth at each stitch than appears natural.

If the rope is merely to give strength to an unsupported awning edge or ridge, you may run it by machine inside a tabling or tape of some sort; see Fig. 4.8.

Fastenings

While we are dealing with hand sewing, I propose reviewing here some of the ways by which canvas can be closed or fastened. I realise that some of these may involve machine sewing, which is not dealt with until the next chapter, but it is better to keep all of them in one place. There are many more systems than those detailed below, but we would be here all night if they were all to be included.

Drawstring (1) Where a drawstring is to be fitted in a tabling, there needs to be room for the cord to emerge at any joining seam. Figure 3.12 shows how this may be achieved without resorting to the finicky removal of a small cut-out of canvas at the seam. Turn over the corner before making the tabling, as shown on the right of the bag seam illustrated; this will not only achieve the desired result, but it will also stop the edge from fraying if it is prone to do so. The tabling is then turned down and sewn in the usual manner, as shown on the left of the bag seam (see also Fig. 6.1). A couple of hand stitches at the start of the seam will add reinforcement to stop it pulling apart.

Fig. 3.12 Drawstring closure

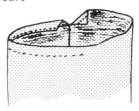

A drawstring needs room at the exit from the tabling for the cord or tape to run freely. This drawing assumes a heat sealed edge; note how the corner is first sewn down (right), then turned when the tabling is sewn (left). Catch the start of the seam itself with a couple of extra stitches to reinforce it, especially if it has been machined.

The depth of tabling or hem will depend on the size of cord to be used, as well as on the weight of canvas of the bag itself (which will help to determine its stiffness). It should not be less than 2–3 cm (1 in), or the drawstring will jam no matter how small the cord or how light the cloth; it may be as much as 7 or 8 cm (3 in) for heavy material. A typical allowance for our purposes would be 4 cm (1½ in), and this is what I frequently suggest.

If you are fitting shock cord inside a tabling, leave a short length protruding until a final fitting, so that you can adjust for tension at the very end.

Drawstring (2) A drawstring may also be run through eyelets which have been punched into the top tabling or hem. Tabling width will depend on eyelet size (you will remember that eyelets should not be fitted on single cloth thickness), which in turn will depend on the cord chosen.

An even number of eyelets must be fitted if the two ends of the cord are to emerge on the same side of the cloth. A look at Fig. 6.1(f) will show that any number of eyelets divisible by four will ensure that cord passes *outside* the bag at the half way point opposite the ties; six or ten would have it pulling inconveniently across the arc of the bag top at its mid point.

Velcro Velcro resists separation better in shear than in peel. In other words, the 'ear flaps' of Fig. 3.13(a) will hold better than the simple closure of (b). There is usually one side which is dictated by circumstances, so that the mating part is better put on second, when the fit may be tested. Like the zipper which follows, velcro is one of the fastenings best put on by machine, but which is included here for convenience.

Fig. 3.13 Velcro closure

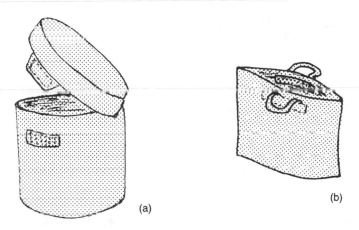

(a)

(b)

Velcro holds better in sheer (a) than in peel (b). If the siting of one part is restricted, as in the 'ear' flaps of (a), sew this on first; the mating part may then be positioned to suit.

Zipper   Marine zippers should be made of Delrin or nylon; the latter absorbs water very slightly. Take care over selection because, though the teeth may not corrode, the slider must be metal (see Chapter 2) and may be vulnerable. If much depends on correct functioning (as with a zipped slab reef in a mainsail), it is worth guarding against breakage by adding a second slider before you start sewing.

If you can't fit the closed zip before the cover or bag is made up, you have to sew it unzipped. Place the two tapes on the outside surface of the fabric, with the teeth pointing *apart*, as shown in Fig. 3.14(a). Stick or pin them in place to prevent creep of one side or the other, then straight stitch them as close to the teeth as you or your machine can go. Turn the zipper under, as in (b) and (c), and sew along the second edge of the zip tape. Finish the ends of a non-separating fastener with a piece of leather or heavy cloth, as shown in (d).

Fig. 3.14 Zipper closure

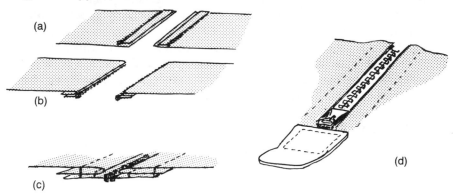

Separate the two halves of the zipper and place them on the outside of the opening, with their teeth pointing *away* from each other, as in (a); pin or stick in position to prevent creep. Sew a single row of straight stitching as close to the teeth as you or your machine can go. Turn the zipper under (b), and sew a second row (c). Finish the ends with a piece of leather or vinyl as in (d).

Lacing hooks   Eyelets and hooks should be fitted completely within a doubled tabling for strength. If you are turning the tabling yourself and you know that eyelets must be fitted, give it the full tuck of Fig. 4.6(c) so that there shall be three thicknesses of cloth for the spur teeth to bite into. The lacing may be loose cord which is tied off after hooking (Fig. 3.15), or else permanently tensioned shock cord pulled across to the hooks. The latter will eventually chafe.

Fig. 3.15 Lacing hooks closure

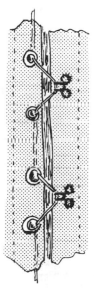

You must have a wide enough tabling to take the hooks and eyelets, preferably with a full tuck to ensure three thicknesses; see Fig. 4.6(c). Lacing will be anchored at one end and tied at the other; shock cord will be sewn at both ends.

Loop-on-loop   Figure 3.16 shows the principle of what is sometimes known as Dutch lacing. It makes a secure closure, often used on tents, but which is somewhat tedious to operate; the usual length of loop is between 10–20 cm (4–8 in). The ends of the cord are best whipped before they are sewn to the canvas, but the very act of sewing will help to hold them from fraying. The last fastening is single, so that it may be tied off to a ring or the tent pole.

Tab hanks   Tab hanks, as shown in Fig. 3.17, may be used to fasten spray dodgers to the guard rail, awnings to ridge poles or, indeed, dinghy jibs to the forestay. The lift-the-dot variety (top) has a sharp stud which may catch awkwardly; the simple press stud (bottom) may therefore be preferred.

Hatch covers   The same two fasteners are shown again in Fig. 3.18, this time in use to hold down a hatch cover. It will be seen that the male portion of both devices can either be clenched to canvas (as in Fig. 3.17), or screwed to wood or fibreglass (as here); you have to specify which you want at the time of buying, of course. Where there is an appropriate purchase, an alternative fastening for a hatch cover would be a simple shock cord in a tabling run right round the hatch coaming. Traditional methods have lashings at the corners, with screw eyes in the woodwork, but these are tedious and the eyes tend to get kicked away.

Fig. 3.16 Loop-on-loop, or Dutch closure

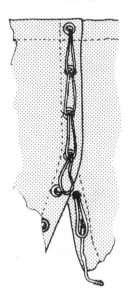

This lacing makes a secure but tedious fastening. Distance between eyelets may be varied, but it is usually somewhere between 10–20 cms (4–8 in). The last lacing is single, so that it may be tied off.

Turnbuttons Known as common sense fasteners in the USA, these twist-lock buttons can either be clenched to canvas or screwed to wood or fibreglass; Fig. 3.19. A weak point of some of these press or turn snaps lies in the spring which may be incorporated in the system. This has been replaced in some fasteners by a rust-free plastic cushion which does the same job.

Tab rings Where a D-ring is going to be subjected to any real strain, it is important to make sure that its join is brazed or welded (or else that the ring is fully forged). Fig. 2.4 shows how such a ring may be attached to canvas by means of a short length of webbing. Where the ring is merely used for a lacing, then this sewing may be done on the machine in a form of cross hatching as in (b); where life and limb depend on it (see Chapter 7 for the bo'sun's chair), make sure that you sew entirely by hand, or else double up the machine stitching with strong hand work at the corners.

Fig. 3.17 Tab hank closure

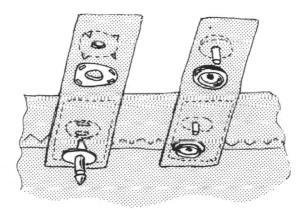

Lift-the-dot fasteners (left) have sharp studs which are vulnerable, so the clenched press stud (right) is usually preferred if knocks are likely.

Fig. 3.18 Stud fastening

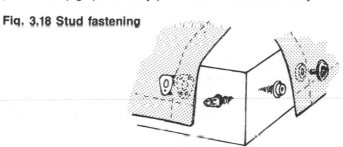

Hatch covers and the like may be held in place by the same two fasteners shown in Fig. 3.17, using the model with the screw fitting stud. Lift-the-dot is more secure, but more vulnerable to damage. Make sure that you fit the female socket to a fully tucked tabling.

Fig. 3.19 Turnbutton fastening

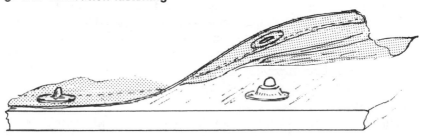

4 Machine Sewing

A large part of your work will be done on the sewing machine – in production terms, that is. You may spend as much *time* on hand work, but it is the machine which produces the quickest results. So it pays to get to know yours.

This book does not set out to be a teaching primer for Mr Howe's invention, but there are one or two points special to working heavy canvas on a domestic machine which will bear reviewing.

Needle and thread

In Chapter 1 thread tensions are mentioned, and there is more below; it is worth repeating briefly here that you should ensure that the link between upper and lower threads lies as near to the middle of the two cloths being sewn as possible; this may not always be possible with heavy material, but take trouble to get the adjustment as good as possible and you will be half-way there.

The other half of the groundwork is to get needle and thread sizes properly matched to the material. Here again, we have already noted some of the parameters, and I can only repeat that you should try to get it right. The margin is wider than you might think, and my local upholsterer uses 110/18 size needles and 40 polyester thread for almost all the work he does, regardless of fabric; but he is ready with even stouter needles if he finds that four plies of thick material make his standard ones break. If you have trouble, consult the maker's instructions and be prepared to vary the sizes.

Synthetic materials are hard on needles and quickly dull their points. Needles are cheap enough, and it is false economy not to throw away anything which becomes blunt.

Thicknesses of cloth

The amount of cloth which you can sew with your machine will depend on the machine itself, on the fabric in question, and on your own skill.

Sewing machine   You should by now have an idea of how well your machine will accept heavy loads. There is a limit to the size of needle and thread you can use, but go as large as you can, taking care not to overload the machine; see Table 3 in Chapter 1.

Fabric   A coarse thick fabric will be more difficult to sew in quantity than a fine, if heavy material. Experience will tell you when you have reached the limit and need to resort to hand sewing.

Skill   Careful operating will break fewer needles than a slap-dash approach, so take trouble and don't pull the cloth about while sewing. If you try to cut corners, you will almost always end by taking longer, as you pause to change a broken needle or to resew a skipped length.

Machine adjustments

Every sewing machine has the same basic adjustments (some of the more sophisticated ones have extra controls dealing with their more numerous functions), which are: foot pressure, needle bar, stitch length, upper thread tension, and lower thread tension. In general, consult the instruction booklet for your particular machine, or else look at a good household sewing manual (I have a friend who likes to quip, 'As a last resort, consult the maker's manual'). The following remarks are for guidance in the specific case of operating a domestic machine with heavy canvas.

Foot pressure   A heavy cloth needs a large needle if it is not to break too often. This will make a correspondingly large hole, with the slight danger that the thread will not be held as the needle is withdrawn on the up stroke; there would then be no loop under the cloth for the shuttle hook to engage at each stitch. This can be cured by increasing the foot pressure. Thick or heavy canvas thus needs greater pressure on the foot, depending on the characteristics of the cloth (a fine weave will hold the thread loop better, so that pressure does not have to be increased so much; a close weave, however, makes withdrawal of the needle more difficult, so that the fabric tends to lift with the needle and once again the loop fails to form, so that more foot pressure is needed in this case). Too much pressure, however, usually makes the bottom cloth gather while the top one slips, thus causing uneven stitches. Too little pressure, on the other hand, allows the work to 'float' under the foot, with loss of guidance and again the danger of uneven stitches, even of a soft fabric being pulled into the bobbin area. The sum of these slightly conflicting, not to say confusing, requirements is usually a need for increased weight on the presser foot when working heavy fabrics.

Needle bar   If the timing is out, the shuttle hook must be adjusted so that it passes close to the eye of the needle at the correct moment. The needle bar is usually adjusted first, then the timing of the shuttle hook. Not all instruction manuals give details, so see your service agent if necessary.

Stitch length   Here again, the coarser or heavier the cloth, the longer each stitch needs to be. But this may be modified according to texture and construction of the fabric. Most heavy canvas needs a big stitch – about 5 mm (³/₁₆ in) long, giving some two stitches per centimetre (5 per in).

Thread tension   As we have seen, the link between the upper and lower threads should be made in the middle of the cloth. This is not always possible with stiff canvas; if it can't be achieved, it should not be allowed on the upper surface. I am indebted to Messrs Singer Sewing Machines for their permission to reproduce the drawings at Figs. 4.1 and 4.2. We agreed in Chapter 1 that it is more effective to increase tension on the side opposite the one where the link lies, than to ease it on the same side as the link (which may only serve to make the whole thing go slack). If the stitch link lies on the upper surface, therefore, tension from the bobbin should be increased as in Fig. 4.1(a), rather than eased from the needle as in Fig. 4.1(b). As it happens, however, it is more likely for a domestic machine working heavy fabrics to suffer from stitch links on the lower surface of the cloth. In this case, cure may be had either by easing the bobbin tension (rather a lengthy exercise, involving a screwdriver) as in Fig. 4.2(a), or by increasing tension on the needle thread – which will often do a better job; Fig. 4.2(b). Fortunately this solution is the easier of the two, so I am happy to report that the more likely of two problems can be better cured by the easier of two solutions.

Faults

Apart from incorrect stitch links, the main faults encountered when sewing heavy canvas on a domestic machine, are needle breakages and skipped stitches. There are others, but they are sufficiently rare for me to refer you once again to your household management book or sewing guide, if the maker's manual doesn't help you.

Needle breakage   The following summary might help to identify your own particular problems:
- (a)   Too fine a needle for the job;
- (b)   You are pulling on the fabric too hard while sewing, rather than allowing the feed dog to do the work;
- (c)   The needle is bent, blunt or incorrectly inserted;
- (d)   Incorrect modes have been selected (zig-zag stitch with straight stitch foot; wrong machine settings).

Fig.4.1 Machine thread tension (1)

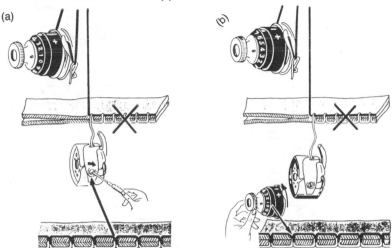

If the stitch link is on top of the work, the best remedy is to increase tension on the lower thread (a); tighten the screw in the spring on the outside of the bobbin case. When sewing coarse canvas, in the unlikely event that you decide to cure the problem by reducing needle thread tension, lower the presser foot and turn the thumb nut adjuster anti-clockwise (b).

Skipped Stitches I include here stitching of erratic length, as well as pulled or missed stitches (if the thread actually breaks, the fault almost certainly lies with the needle; check for correct size, installation, cleanliness or sharpness). Principal causes are:

(a) Foot pressure is insufficient for heavy canvas, so that a loop is not being formed for the shuttle hook to engage;

(b) Wrong size of needle;

(c) Needle is wrongly inserted, bent or dirty;

(d) The bobbin is too tightly (or too loosely) wound, or its mechanism is dirty;

(e) You are pulling too hard on the fabric while sewing, rather than allowing the feed dog to do the work;

(f) The feed dog is dirty, so that it does not grip properly;

(g) Loops on the surface (upper or lower) indicate faulty threading of the machine; check bobbin seating (for upper loops), or the feed to the tension discs (for lower loops);

(h) The thread is brittle so that it sticks. Put some PTFE or silicone lubricant on a felt pad (not too much) and tape it to the machine where the thread will run over it as it feeds to the needle.

Fig. 4.2 Machine thread tension (2)

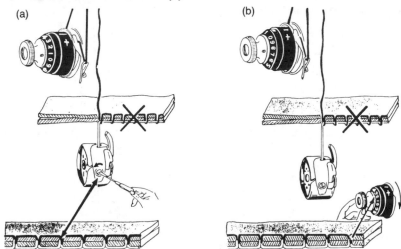

The more common fault with heavy canvas is for the stitch link to be underneath the work; you may attempt a cure by easing tension on the lower thread (a), through loosening the screw in the spring on the outside of the bobbin case. But it is both easier and usually more effective with heavy canvas to increase tension on the needle thread (b). Lower the presser foot and turn the thumb nut adjuster clockwise.

Types of machine stitch

A sewing machine forms a continuous chain of stitches, so that a broken thread anywhere means that a whole length of stitching comes loose. For this reason, the start and finish of a row should be anchored by over-sewing a short length in reverse. If you are sewing vinyl, however, do not make unnecessary holes by backstitching; do what you have to do with any cloth when your machine can't reverse – leave enough unsewn thread to enable the ends to be tied off.

Zig-zag It is conventional to assume that all canvas work shall be tackled with a zig-zag stitch – indeed, many sailmakers now use a form of stepped zig-zag, whereby three zig-zag stitches are sewn at 45 degrees to the main line of a seam, and then the next three at 45 degrees the other side of the line, before switching again in a zig-zag of zig-zags. The zig-zag itself stems from using rather hard fabric for sails, so that some give in the seam is necessary to absorb possible movement of the material in use. Zig-zag formation also enables the machinist to sew 'on-and-off' a sealed edge, which helps prevent fraying which may occur due to faulty sealing – but consistent accuracy is necessary.

Straight stitch A zig-zag facility is not essential. We are not going to use a very stiff polyester cloth, so the give will be in the material and not the stitching. Therefore, an uncomplicated straight stitch will be faster than one which darts from side to side. Jim Grant, American sailmaker and owner of Sailrite Kits® (the Indiana mail-order firm coupled with his sailmaking school) goes so far as to say in his book (under References at the end) that, where cloths are folded or tucked under to prevent fraying, the straight stitch is stronger. There is not much in it, but it is nice to know that you may still use your old machine which can only sew in a straight line.

Machine seaming

Seaming is the basic process of joining the elements of two panels of cloth together, and should be mastered competently. You will find that many seams start with the two cloths lying on top of one another (often, though not always, with their outsides touching), and the work is unfolded either at the end or during the course of sewing.

Pro's and con's Before going into seaming in detail, let us briefly review some of the advantages and disadvantages of mechanisation, obvious though they may seem. The slight drawbacks are:

(a) Machine thread is lighter than hand twine, so it degrades more readily if exposed to sunlight or chafe;

(b) A machine cannot sew through as many thicknesses as can be tackled by hand, nor can it always get to awkward or bulky seams;

(c) One break in the thread puts a lot of stitching in danger.

Having said that, machining has the following advantages over the more traditional hand work:

(a) Because it is so much quicker, it will enable you to make good progress on the job. This can help maintain a beginner's enthusiasm, because it shows that an end product is getting nearer;

(b) It is neater than hand sewing;

(c) It is more accurate.

Seam allowance It is a good idea to get used to a basic seam allowance, or width, which is used whenever nothing wider is called for (in our work, a broad seam may be required to carry eyelets, or to give a base on which to add reinforcement tape). Many sewing machines have guidelines in inches or millimetres etched on the needle plate; if yours does not, then draw some with a felt-tip pen, or stick some adhesive tape on the plate.

Round seam Though this is more akin to the hand tacking stitch of Fig. 3.1(b) than the round seam of Fig. 3.4, like the latter this is the quickest and easiest of them all. Match the two edges to be joined, outside surfaces touching, and run a row of straight stitching (not zig-zag) 1 cm ($\frac{1}{4}$ – $\frac{1}{2}$ in) inside the edges of the panels; Fig. 4.3(a). Open the result and, if you want better waterproofing, or improved strength (as with an awning ridge), or more neatness on the inside surface, sew a length of tape along the flaps; Fig. 4.3(b).

Fig. 4.3 Round seam (machine)

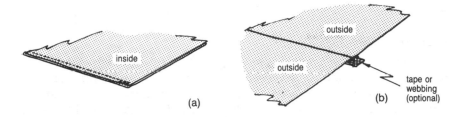

inside

(a)

outside

outside

tape or
webbing
(optional)

(b)

Place the two panels on top of each other, outside surfaces touching and edges aligned (a). Fix with transfer tape if desired, and machine with straight stitching inside the edges. Open out and, if neatness, proofing, or more strength is required, sew a length of tape over the flaps (b).

Flat seam   This is achieved in exactly the same manner as the hand-sewn flat seam of Fig. 3.5. Lay the two panels together, using double-sided sticky tape to hold them steady, and machine with a zig-zag or straight stitch, whichever you prefer. If you use a zig-zag, what is known as 'all-on' gives a stronger result than 'on-and-off'; Fig. 4.4. If you have to tuck the edges under, there are special presser-foot attachments which will make this easier, or you can rub the edge down to crease it in place.

Fig. 4.4 Flat seam (machine)

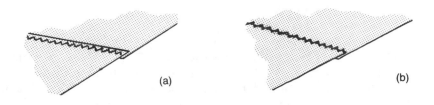

(a)

(b)

Overlap the panels as in (a) and sew with a zig-zag stitch for appearance, "all-on". Turn the work over and run along the other edge, "on-and-off" if you trust your accuracy. Catch the ends with a couple of hand stitches.

Flat-felled seam Unlike the hand-sewn flat-felled seam of Fig. 3.6, this can be achieved on the machine in one step, if transfer tape is used. Stick one cloth on another, with 1 cm (¼–½ in) overlap, and with similar sides touching (outside or inside); Fig. 4.5(a). Crease the bottom flap with a rubbing iron (scissors or knife handle), and stick it down (b). Fold the top cloth right across the future seam, rub it down to crease it, and then sew both sides of the seam with either straight or zig-zag stitching (c). The result looks the same from either side, and is probably the most waterproof of all.

Fig. 4.5 Flat-felled seam (machine)

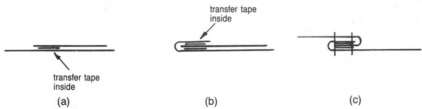

transfer tape
inside

transfer tape
inside

(a)   (b)   (c)

This can be achieved in one operation if transfer tape is used. Lay one panel on the other with similar sides touching, and with an overlap (a). Then fold the bottom cloth over, and crease it with a rubbing iron (b) onto a second strip of transfer tape. Fold the top panel over as shown in (c) and rub it down, before sewing along both edges with straight or zig-zag stitches.

Tabling A tabling is as easily sewn by machine as it is by hand (Fig. 3.7), except that the machine is much quicker. When turning the edge to form a tabling, there are three options:

(a)   Single turn, leaving selvedge or heat-sealed edge in the open; Fig. 4.6(a). This is simple, but can only be safely done if the edge will not fray;

(b)   Turn the flap, with edge tucked under to prevent the cloth fraying, or if a drawstring will be fitted; Fig. 4.6(b);

(c)   Turn the flap, with edge fully tucked under to provide treble thickness strength throughout, for attaching eyelets, hooks etc; Fig. 4.6(c).

Use transfer tape or rub down to crease the tabling, and sew along both sides. Somehow a zig-zag stitch looks more aesthetic here, but that may be only my opinion stemming from my years in the sailmaking business; a straight stitch is perfectly acceptable. If the edge of the cloth takes a curve, so that any tabling would also be curved, there will be a multitude of small wrinkles; Fig. 4.7(a). Depending on the amount of curve and flexibility of the cloth to accommodate it, you may find it easier to sew a more pliable tape long the unturned edge; Fig. 4.7(b).

Fig. 4.6 Machined tabling

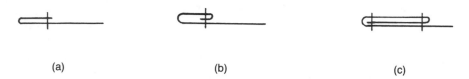

(a)   (b)   (c)

There are four types of tabling open to us; the above three and that of Fig. 4.7 below.
(a)   The simple tabling may be used where the raw edge had been heat sealed (compare Fig. 3.7). It is quickest, but offers the least strength of the three.
(b)   If the edge may fray, or if a drawstring will be added, the tabling should be tucked under before sewing. Make sure that your stitching catches the edge inside.
(c)   Where eyelets or stud fasteners will be added, the tabling should be given a full tuck for extra strength.

Fig. 4.7 Curved tabling

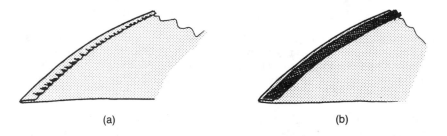

(a)   (b)

Where a curved edge is involved, a multitude of small wrinkles will arise (a) unless the turned edge is cut off and replaced in traditional sailmaking style; this is a tedious process, open to error by the amateur, and I won't bother you with it here (see *Sails* if you must know about it). If the curve is not too marked, a flexible tape may be sewn to the heat sealed edge (b).

Machine roping

If a long run of rope is needed along an edge, you will make a quicker, and probably neater, job of it by machining it inside a tape; Fig. 4.8. While the rope does not add a great deal to the edge's strength when put on in this manner, the tape will do so. If strength is all that is needed, therefore, omit the rope altogether and just put on the tape. If, however, you need the rope to run in a groove of some sort (such as a sun awning along the edge of a caravan or trailer roof, or in some sort of spar to help it spread), then include the correct size of rope for the purpose.

A tape 5 cm (2 in) wide should be folded along its length, and the two parts of tape stapled together reasonably close around the rope. Draw a pencil line tight up against the rope, where the first row of stitching will go. If your machine will not sew close enough, you either have to sew it by hand, using the straight tacking stitch of Fig. 3.1(b), or else resort to subterfuge. Withdraw the rope, pulling a small messenger line behind it (if you lose the messenger, work it through using a tapestry needle as a bodkin). Now the machine will get at the smaller bulk quite happily.

When the machined row is complete, use the messenger to pull the original rope back into the tube you have just created. Your machining needs to be accurate, because you won't get the rope back inside the tape if you stray the wrong side of your pencil line.

You may now machine the taped rope to the edge concerned, putting half the tape each side of the main fabric; Fig. 4.8(a).

Fig. 4.8 Machined roping

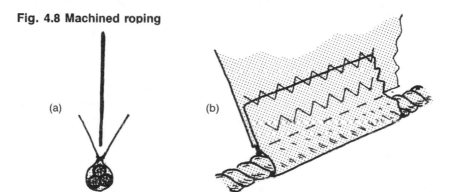

(a)   (b)

Fold a tape round the rope and machine with a straight stitch close alongside it. If you do not have a special roping adaptor for the foot of your machine (and who, apart from the professional, has?), you won't be able to get near enough. Fold the rape round the rope, mark the correct line for stitching, then set the rope aside and enclose a thinner cord instead, while you machine to your line. Now use the cord as a messenger to pull the full-size rope through.

Machined fasteners

Most fasteners are best put on by hand, velcro and zippers being two of the exceptions. They are, however, also capable of being fitted by hand, so I have included them in Chapter 3 in order to keep them with all the other fasteners. Seek there and ye shall find.

5 Care and Repair

If you are going to make your own covers, awnings or tarpaulins, you should also know how to look after them. That means care in use, and repair in abuse.

Care Not Cure

That prevention is better than cure is old hat, but none the less true for that. This means taking care not to maltreat any hatch covers, sail coats or, indeed, kitbags and the like.

Chafe

Chafe is a big problem with sails, because when they are set there is movement on the boat so that the danger is always there. The problem is not present to quite the same degree with covers because, in general terms, most things which are covered are *ipso facto* static. But there can still be chafe where a hatch has sharp corners, or an outboard has an awkward lever under its cover. Even then, there will not usually be a great deal of movement, and the trouble is more likely to occur when an outside agent is introduced: lazy jacks rubbing on a sail coat, a liferaft container rocking against a hatch cover, or spinnaker sheets running under guardrail spray dodgers.

Another source of wear is a loose lashing on a vehicle tilt, so that the airflow can get hold of a corner and quickly flog it to death unless speedy action is taken. The watchword is 'speedy'.

Make a point of marking any new cover with a pencil at likely chafe points as soon as it is fitted; then apply reinforcement patches as soon as possible. From time to time check all machine stitching (which sits proud of the cloth and is thus vulnerable), and be particularly careful with any acrylic covers, because the material wears more quickly than cotton or polyester.

Cotton

Most of us know that cotton will attract mildew if it is put away wet, but I would be failing in my duty if I did not mention it again. In addition, coloured cotton tends to fade in sunlight, but the strength does not go until wear sets in. If cotton is used in a damp environment, or at sea, wash it occasionally and try to see that it is always allowed to dry out.

Cotton can be proofed after it has been made up into a cover. It is a messy process, best left to the experts, but well worth considering, as it prolongs active life.

Polyester

Terylene and Dacron are virtually unaffected by most mild domestic chemicals, including weak acids (but see below under *Cleaning* for the effect of alkalis). The real killer is sunlight (and some industrial smoke), which can render a medium polyester as brittle as paper in a season's constant exposure, unless it has been specially inhibited against ultraviolet attack. I am not advocating that you should cover your covers, but sometimes they may have to be considered as throw-away goods for the protection of the more valuable items they are shielding. Wash out any salt, before storing for the winter in a dry environment.

Nylon

Nylon behaves in much the same way as polyester – it is, however, usually much thinner and therefore more subject to degradation; this is accelerated by acidity (see *Cleaning* below). Nylon is easy to dry after being washed, so there can be no excuse for dirty windscoops or curtains.

Acrylic

Acrylic is more resistant to ultraviolet rays than polyester or nylon. It will soak up water unless it has been treated with Scotchgard or a similar preparation and, while the wet fabric will not suffer from mildew attack, the tiny particles of dirt usually trapped in any weave will act as hosts. The moral is wash regularly, and keep it dry if possible – vain advice if it forms a winter cover, but at least see that it gets good air circulation.

PVC-coated cloth

Polyvinylchloride coating is used frequently to provide waterproofing to a woven fabric – for our purposes, this usually means polyester or nylon. Its very success means that air permeability is zero, which promotes condensation, so take such covers off from time to time and allow the air to blow through.

If you have found a cheap cloth, it may be that it is because poor materials have been used, or manufacturing processes skimped. These can manifest themselves in cracking of the shiny surface, until the chemicals start to run off as a milky liquid when it rains; the cloth may also discolour or become sticky. There is no cure other than to make a new one of better fabric.

Duradon

Duradon® is an all-synthetic tarpaulin fabric, which looks and feels like heavy flax or cotton. Developed some twenty years ago for the road haulage industry, it is composed of a blend of nylon and polyester fibres, proofed by a dry chemical process. The cloth will 'breathe' so that condensation is minimised, yet it does not leak under normal use (seepage can occur if water is allowed to collect in pools and cause hollow loading).

Duradon comes in two weights, the heavier of which would present the average domestic sewing machine with problems if more than one or two thicknesses were involved. It has been so successful that the tan-coloured variety is used extensively for sails for traditional craft such as Thames barges or other large trading vessels. Its use for our purposes, of course, is for large clamp covers or lorry tilts.

Cleaning

Clean covers not only look better than dirty ones; they also last longer. It makes sense to tackle any stains as soon as they appear, because you will then have a better chance of remembering what it was that caused the stain in the first place.

Synthetic fibres do not swell when wet so, if waterproofing is required, they have to be specially treated at the production stage. Where this treatment involves a dry chemical process (as in a fabric such as Duradon, which needs to breathe yet remain waterproof), the cloth must not be washed in soap or detergent, otherwise the proofing will be irreparably damaged. But dirt in the weave will allow damp to penetrate due to a process called 'wicking', whereby moisture seeps through the weave via the dirt, in a manner reminiscent of osmosis of ill repute. Washing should be restricted to plain water.

ICI Fibres have published a pamphlet for over twenty years now, called *Laundering and Dry Cleaning of Terylene Sails*, which they have allowed me to reproduce in full, or to quote, in my various books on sails. The pamphlet deals specifically with white Terylene sailcloth (dyed sails should be dealt with by specialists), but is full of good advice and specifies the treatment needed to remove many of the stains commonly encountered on sails. The preceding paragraph about not washing Duradon in soap to avoid spoiling its waterproofing, shows that ICI's advice should be carried forward to covers with care. But common sense should see you through if you proceed slowly.

Most polyester (and nylon) sailcloth will wash well in hot water and detergent. A caveat here – acids accelerate the degrading effects of sunlight on nylon, and alkalis do the same for polyester. When a pH test paper is dipped into the detergent, it changes colour and can be held against a graded chart; pH.7 is exactly neutral, with values below 7 becoming progressively more acidic, and those above being more alkaline. Some soap powders are alkali-based, but liquid detergents (being often of the 'soapless' variety) are less likely to be so. Some cloths react worse to these detergents and other solvents than others; PVC coatings and most dry chemical proofing processes, for instance, may come away from their weave under certain conditions. If in doubt, seek professional advice from the cloth manufacturers, taking care to be specific as to the precise fabric and stain in question.

When cleaning with chemicals, treat all fumes as both flammable and noxious, and you should not come to much harm (plenty of fresh air, and no smoking – apart from anything else, chlorinated solvents produce phosgene gas when inhaled through a lighted cigarette!). Always use stainless steel or polythene containers (or enamel, if there are no chips in it to allow ferrous particles to come in contact with whatever chemicals you are using).

Repairs

As I have said elsewhere, a stitch in time was never more likely to save nine than when repairing sails (or canvas goods of any kind, for that matter). Much of what follows in this chapter will be known already to those who are used to repairing their own sails; this chapter only scratches the surface. Those who want fuller details are referred to one of my other books on the subject.

Repairs to machine stitching
A sail may chafe at the leech tabling or at certain seams, so that a complete line of worn stitching needs to be oversewn. Fortunately, this doesn't concern us here; nevertheless, there can be occasions when a longish run

of stitching on a cover is broken or frayed at intervals, so that the entire length is suspect. This is most likely to occur as a result of long exposure to the sun, which would cause the synthetic thread to weaken (a sun awning or a sail coat in the tropics are obvious candidates).

Seam repairs by machine   If the entire awning or sail coat can be got under the arm of the sewing machine, run a third row of stitching down the middle of the two weakened rows in question. Beware of blocking any drawstring or batten pocket which may run across the seam.

Seam repairs by hand   If the job won't go under the sewing machine, or if you haven't got one handy, you are saddled with a complete seam to sew by hand – but if this has to be done on deck in the tropics, you won't mind will you? Sew from side to side using the tacking stitch of Fig. 3.1(b) and picking up the old machine stitch holes. This is not only for a neater appearance, but also because you will run less risk of pulling the original shape out of true; Fig. 5.1. One pass along the seam is enough. It will leave alternate stitches unfilled on either side of the canvas, but the hand twine you use will be more than double the strength of the original machine thread. The only reason for going back over it again is for appearance, so don't bother unless you (or your spouse) are fussy.

Fig. 5.1 Hand repairs to machine stitching

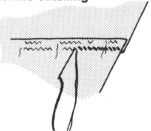

Pick up the old machine holes, not only for looks, but also to avoid pulling the seam out of shape. There is no need to go over the run twice to fill in the gaps left at alternate stitches because your hand twine will be more than double the strength of the original thread.

Darning

The domestic darn is usually different from what the sailmaker calls a darn, which is different again according to whether it is done by hand or machine. So I shall describe all three.

Domestic darn   Only used by the canvas worker on holes small enough to have been caused by a lighted cigarette, or by a minor case of point chafing (anything larger should be patched), this darn adopts the familiar pattern of crossed twines, running over and under alternate threads in the domestic manner. As with darning a sock, make sure that you start and finish each row in sound material.

Sailmaker's hand darn   The hand-worked sailmaker's darn employs the herringbone stitch of Fig. 3.8. Used afloat, it effects a temporary repair to a sail which must continue to do duty; Fig. 5.2. The canvas worker will find less occasion for its services as such, and he or she normally only uses it to pull a tear together so that a decent patch may be put on (see Fig. 5.4 below). Make sure that you sew into sound material, and don't pull the stitches too tight or you will cause wrinkles. If this somewhat tenuous repair is to be used on its own, it can be strengthened by covering with adhesive repair tape – but you are then half-way to a patch, so what's stopping you?

Fig. 5.2 Sailmaker's darn (hand)

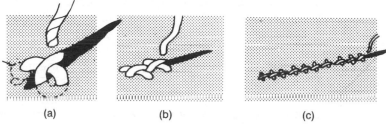

| (a) | (b) | (c) |

Use of the herringbone stitch described in Fig. 3.8 produces what the sailmaker calls his darn. It should not be pulled too tight, and may be assisted by sticking repair tape over the finished job. Its principal use afloat is to cobble up a tear until a better job can be effected; we only need it to hold a rip together temporarily while a patch is being put on (Fig. 5.4).

Machine darn   This is an extremely temporary repair and, if you have bothered to get the sewing machine out at all, you might as well do the job properly and patch the hole. It might just be acceptable to apply it to a short clean cut which needs to be stopped from spreading. Using as wide a zig-zag as convenient, run a row of stitches along the cut, so that the zig-zag takes in both sides with alternate stitches; Fig. 5.3. You can see that there is not much room for inaccuracy (nor for frayed cloth edges which would give poor holding ground). Again, a strip of repair tape, applied before or after sewing, would not come amiss – it needs all the help it can get.

Patches

If a tear or hole is too big to be mended by herringboning the edges together as described above, it will have to be patched. Pull the tear

Fig. 5.3 Machine darn

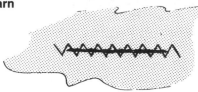

I shouldn't be pandering to the lazy by showing you this. If you are getting the machine out at all, you might as well patch any cut properly. There might just be an excuse to apply this to a very short cut which has clean edges which will not fray. The zig-zag must, of course, be wide enough to straddle the cut, and must be accurate.

temporarily together with sticky tape, a few tacking stitches or, indeed, the sailmaker's darn. Draw a rectangle where the patch will go, and cut a piece of similar cloth to fit (with its threadlines following those of the cover); allow for turning under if the new cloth cannot be heat sealed and is likely to fray, as in Fig. 5.4(b).

Offer the patch to the cover, and see that it is fairly slack; pin it in place, or use transfer tape if it will hold. Sew round the edges of the patch with the tabling stitch as in (b). Turn the work over and trim the tear to a rectangle, 2.5 cm (1 in) or so inside the rectangle of stitching, heat sealing as you go; if it won't heat seal, allow for mitre-cutting into the corners and turning under as in (c). Table round this new edge and the job is complete; Fig. 5.4(d).

Fig. 5.4 Patching

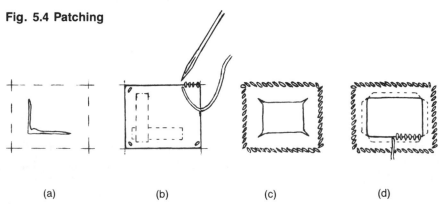

| (a) | (b) | (c) | (d) |

Pull the edges of the tear together with a darn (Fig. 5.1), draw round the outside of the patch you propose (a), pin or tack the patch in place (b), and sew round the outside by hand or machine. Turn the job over and trim the tear to a rectangle, rather smaller than the stitching, heat sealing as you go. If you can't heat seal, allow for mitre-cutting into the corners and tucking under. Sew round again, and the job is complete (d).

Re-roping

Even if you have never sewn a rope by hand before, if a short length has come unstitched from, say, the corner of a big tilt, make with the palm. Generations of dyed-in-the-wool sailmakers will turn in their graves when I write the solecism: 'Hand roping is a piece of cake.'

Before a million ghostly bench workers rise from their tombs to zero in on my bedroom in the chill of the dog watches, I should qualify that by adding: 'if it's only a question of catching a dozen stitches which have broken or come undone.'

This presupposes that the rope was put on by hand in the first place. It will then merely be a question of seeing where it lies naturally against the canvas, and using the roping stitch described in Chapter 3. Start about three strands into good stitching, and work towards the free end (if one is hanging loose); this avoids any problems with having to finish exactly right, to avoid a shortfall of rope or a surplus when you reach the sound stitching; Fig. 3.11. The error you are most likely to make is to pull your stitches too tight, which might cause a slight pucker. But the result is most satisfying. You can now do roping.

If the original sewing was right through the rope by special machine, you may decide either to pick up the old machine stitch holes by hand (possibly right through the rope, or possibly involving tape), or else to sew between the lay of the strands in the traditional manner. Each case will have to be decided on its own merits; see Fig. 4.8 for details of machine roping.

Torn eyelets

If a punched eyelet has pulled out, you have four options:
  (a) Tidy up the canvas and punch in a larger eyelet;
  (b) Hand work a proper eye, probably slightly larger than the one which has pulled out;
  (c) Patch the offending area and punch or sew a new eyelet or eye of the same size as the original;
  (d) Consider fitting a D-ring with tape as in Fig. 2.4.

The fact that the eyelet has pulled out is a strong indication that the stresses are too great for a punched replacement. If it is a hand-sewn eye which has pulled, you will almost certainly have to adopt option (c) or (d). Whatever you do, don't try to re-use a bent or deformed eyelet, unless you want it to pull straight out again.

Broken hooks, rings, etc.

Examine the broken fitting to establish the cause of the breakage; in order of likelihood, this will be:

(a)   Too small a fitting. Replace with a size larger;

(b)   Torn canvas. Patch before replacement;

(c)   Defective fitting; replace. If it is a D-ring, check that the replacement is a one-piece job, rather than one with an unwelded join.

Windows

Most window material (in cockpit spray dodgers, tent flaps, etc.) will deteriorate through weathering. Like many synthetic cloths, it will become brittle to the point where it cracks and tears away. If the surrounding canvas is in sound heart, so that it is worth replacing (doubtful this, because the same weathering process will have acted on the cloth), spread it out on the floor and double check. Unpick the stitching which holds the window in place (it may be sewn direct to the canvas, but is more likely to have a strip of cloth or tape holding it down).

The problem you will face, and which did not confront the person who first fitted the window, is one of distortion of the 'frame' (the window will originally have been sewn before any canvas was cut out as an opening). You now have to spread the area flat, ensuring that it lies evenly. When this has been done to your satisfaction, offer up the sheet of window material and cut it roughly to size. Fix it with tape or staples, and then hold up the result to check for fit. Once you are satisfied, mark the final size of the window with chinagraph pencil or felt-tip pen. If you think you can trim it after it has been machined in place, sew it without disturbing the tape or staples. If you have to remove it to cut it to the correct size, give it some match marks, so that you will be able to find the same even spread when you put it back; see Fig. 6.12.

You are now in business, and it is a question of machining everything in place once you are satisfied that you have a good fit.

Whippings

Ropes, lines and cords used for lashings have a distressing tendency to fray at the ends, even if they have been heat sealed at some time. Whippings put on last year come undone, let alone those which have served for several seasons. Rubber collars perish.

You need worry no more, because you are about to learn how to put on a whipping which will last – for ever.

Bold words, I hear you say, as you bet it won't. But hear me out, and you will be drawing your old age pension before this whipping comes apart (depending on how old you are now, he adds prudently). Seriously though, this is a toughie, which will withstand a lot of harsh treatment. It's called the *sailmaker's whipping*.

Sailmaker's whipping   You need a light seaming twine (say, 2 lb) or a heavy machine thread (V.69), depending on the size of rope you are going to whip. Thread a needle with two parts, wax it and knot the end. Start about three diameters from the end of the rope, and sew through the lay of the strands to hide the stopper knot and get a firm base. Whip against the lay as normal, working from left to right and towards the free end of the rope. Take care to see that the two parts of twine lie evenly side by side without twists, and close up against the previous turn. Many reference books advise that the distance covered should be equal to the diameter of the rope; but we want this to last, so we will make it two diameters. The final turn should thus be a diameter from the free end.

When the full number of turns have been put on, sew through between the lay of the strands (some advise that this should be done diagonally, to come out at the starting or left end, if the rope's resistance is not too great); Fig. 5.5(a). Run the twine along the groove of the lay to the other end of the whipping, and sew between the next two strands, then back along the next groove to sew through again, and finally repeat for the third

Fig. 5.5 Sailmaker's whipping

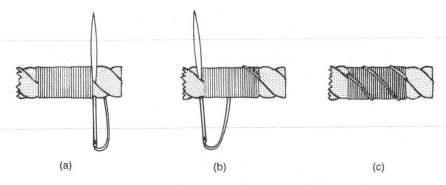

(a)   (b)   (c)

Sew through the lay of the rope about three diameters from the end and whip in the usual way towards the free end of the rope (against the lay). Take care to see that the two parts of twine lie close together without twists and close against the previous turns (a). When you have covered a distance equal to two diameters, sew through the lay (some authorities suggest that this should be diagonally, to come out at the starting end, but this can be difficult and I don't consider it necessary). Run the twine along the groove of the lay over the top of your whipping (b), and then sew it between two strands at the far end. When you have done this three times, repeat the process for extra security and then sew through before cutting off (c).

groove; Fig. 5.5(b). If your twine is not too thick, repeat the whole process to double up the holding turns, before sewing through and cutting off; Fig. 5.5(c).

American whipping   This is not the drubbing given on Lake Champlain to the Royal Navy by the Revolting Colonials in the 1812 affair. It is a method of securing a whipping by tying its two ends in the middle; Fig. 5.6. Lay the starting end of the twine (black end in (a) and (b) in the figure) along the rope pointing towards the right, and cover it with two thirds of the turns you will need to complete the job; leave sufficient twine on the starting end to tie a knot. Lay the working end of the twine (arrowed in the figure) along the rope, pointing towards the left and with a loop hanging free. Take the remaining turns round the rope and over the working end (but leaving the starting end free). Pull each turn tight and ease its twists as you go (c). Draw the working end through to make all taut, and tie off in a reef knot; Fig. 5.6(d).

Fig. 5.6 American whipping

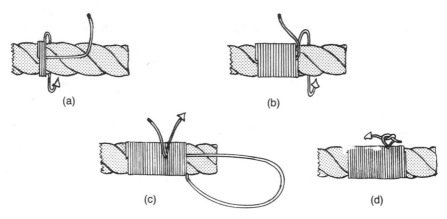

(a)

(b)

(c)

(d)

The black end of twine is the inert or starting end, and is allowed to run out enough to knot later (b). The arrow is the working end, which is looped to lie under the finishing turns (c). When all is pulled tight, the two ends are tied off (d).

West Country whipping   This is an altogether different whipping and, though it can be clapped on more quickly (and therefore useful if you have little time) and, like the American Whipping, without the need for a needle, it is not so neat as the others. Middle the twine at the start point and take half a turn with each end; tie a single overhand knot. Take another half turn and tie again. Repeat until the equivalent of one diameter has been covered, then tie off with a full reef knot.

Seizings

A seizing is a whipping which seizes two lines together, or two wires, or a line and a spar. The principles are the same, except that you will not always be able to secure it with the sailmaker's holding turns described above. The same effect can be achieved with what are known as frapping turns, twisted together to finish off. A child can do it – in fact, it was small cabin boys who used to seize or nip the anchor cable of the old sailing men o' war to the endless capstan hawser, as anchor was weighed, the two cables had to be parted and nipped together again each time the seizing reached the end of the loop as the hook came up. Not surprisingly, the boys came to be known as nippers.

Racking seizing When two ropes need to be seized so that considerable strains may be transferred, a racking seizing is clapped on (as with whippings and, indeed, extra sail, a seizing is usually said to be 'clapped on' – but please don't ask me why). Figure-of-eight turns are taken round the two ropes; Fig. 5.7(a). Riding turns round both ropes then fill the gaps as in (b). A couple of frapping turns are clapped on to haul it all tight, and the end is half-hitched, tucked or sewn through; Fig. 5.7(c).

Fig. 5.7 Racking seizing

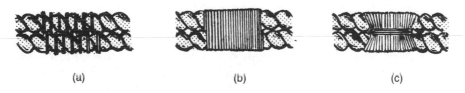

(a)   (b)   (c)

Take figure-of-eight turns round and between the two ropes of, say, an eye splice (a). Cover these turns with full riding turns right round both ropes (b) to fill the gaps. Finally, clap on two or three frapping turns (for some reason, a seizing is always said to be clapped on) to haul it all tight (c). Half-hitch, tuck or sew off.

Sails

Once you have started on canvas repairs, if you are a boat owner you will want to try your hand on a few sails as well. This book, however, is not about sails, although working on them makes an excellent introduction to the mysteries of the sailmaker's palm. If this is your scene, get my book on sail repair. Alternatively, I can recommend a cheap booklet on the subject, which was put out by the *Practical Boat Owner* magazine in 1980. Read either work, but you would not expect me to prefer another's short summary of my own more complete treatment of the subject.

6 Simple Projects

We shan't get anywhere unless we start *making* something soon. This chapter details a number of relatively uncomplicated jobs, which will be fairly quick to finish and thus encouraging to the beginner. You will find that they are useful as well.

Ditty Bag

Design

A small tool hold-all for needles, palm, fid, scissors, beeswax and the like will always be welcomed by the canvas worker, so a ditty bag is first to figure on our projects list. It will be quick and simple to make, and offers good practice in both sewing and eyelet fitting.

Material   A ditty bag may be made of virtually any material. Man-made fabrics can be heat sealed at the edges to prevent fraying, and will thus be easier to work, but in this case I shall assume that cotton is the choice; the various seams will therefore need to be tucked under to stop them unravelling. Fig. 6.1. gives suggested sizes, but these may of course be altered to suit.

Manufacture

We shall use a mixture of machine and hand sewing, if only to give practice in both skills.

Tabling   The first stitching should be the top hem, which should be machine sewn as a 4 cm (1½ in) tabling. If you propose to fit a drawstring inside, treat the corners as advised in Fig. 3.12 by folding and sewing them as in Fig. 6.1(a), before folding the tabling proper (having tucked its edge under) as in (b). This corner tucking does not need to be done if eyelets are proposed as in (f), but a full tuck for the tabling as illustrated in Fig. 4.6(c) would then be advisable, in order to provide greater strength for the ring teeth of the eyelet to grip.

Fig. 6.1 Ditty Bag

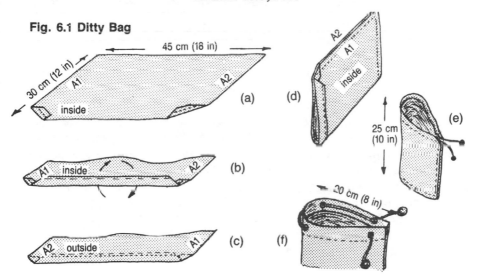

If a drawstring is to be fitted, fold and sew the top corners as in (a), then fold the tabling over and sew it along its extreme edge (b). Now turn the panel over as in (c) and mate the two seam edges A1 and A2 as in (d). Sew down the side and along the bottom as a round seam (by hand as Fig. 3.4, or by machine as Fig. 4.3). The bag is now turned right side out and the drawstring added (e). If eyelets are to be fitted, four or eight will ensure that the cord passes **outside** the bag opposite the tie-point, thus helping to hold it closed (f).

Centre seam   Having finished the tabling by machine, reverse the panel so that the outside is on top (c), mate the two edges A_1-A_2 so that the work is inside out as in (d), and machine sew a round seam as in Fig. 4.3. Continue round the bottom corner and along the base. If you mitre-cut the bottom corner to make it easier, you will leave a slightly weak point which may develop into a small hole later; crimping the cloth and sewing it all together will be more secure (though possibly not so neat). As this seam will be inside the bag and not so open to chafe, it is not essential to turn the edges under to stop them fraying but, if you want to be correct, you have to go round again each side, in order to tuck and sew down the edges.

Drawstring   The bag should now be turned the right way out, a couple of hand stitches added to anchor the top of the seam, and the drawstring threaded with a bodkin, or a messenger sent down on a tapestry needle (e). If you decide on eyelets as in Fig. 6.1(f) – four should be enough – the tabling process would be more straightforward (no need to turn the corners, or to ensure that the ends of the tube remain unsewn when seaming).

Canvas Worker's Tool Roll

Design

Both amateur canvas worker and DIY sailmaker would probably prefer to keep his or her tools in a special canvas roll, rather than in a simple ditty bag of the kind we have just seen, where everything will get mixed up together. The roll shown at Fig. 6.2 is one which I originally devised for my own sail repair kit; in slightly modified form we eventually sold quite a few when I was working first for Ratsey & Lapthorn at Cowes, and then later for W.G. Lucas & Son at Portsmouth.

Material A tool roll may be made of medium-weight cotton 200 gms (6 oz), but this will involve extra work as every edge would need to be turned under to prevent fraying. Any fairly soft man-made fabric will do, even off-cuts of reject cloth. You will also need a short length of thin cord, some velcro, and a strip of elastic ribbon (as opposed to shock cord).

Manufacture

Cut a piece of fabric to the overall sizes shown in Fig. 6.2(a), and draw a half-way line across the middle at A-A. Sew 35 cm (14 in) of 2–4 cm (1–1½ in) wide elastic ribbon to the inside of the panel in the position indicated, making sure that the inner end overlaps the half-way line you drew by 1 cm (½ in). Sew only across the width of the elastic, close to each end, and then make further divisions as indicated in detail at (b); these will provide strops for tools and bottles to be pushed through. The smallest gaps will ensure that small tools will be at the edge of the roll, thus making for a neater packet when filled; the largest division will just hold a sewing palm, so leave it at the outside of the roll in order that you shall not have to fold the flap at that point.

Tabling Cut and heat seal across the tabling allowance of 2.5 cm (1 in) at A and A. What I call the flap end (with the elastic) is next tabled all round up to these cuts, making a 2.5 cm (1 in) hem. Do the same across the other (pocket) *end*, but leave the sides unsewn (they will be seamed together). If you wish, you may decide to fit one strip of velcro at the same time as this last tabling; see next paragraph.

Velcro The tool roll will have its pocket held shut by velcro, and now is the time to fit it. Sew one strip on the inside of the panel alongside the half-way line, but just on the pocket end side of it; if it runs across one end of the elastic, it makes a neat job, as shown in (b). Fold the pocket end in half along B-B (right side out), so that its tabling coincides with the strip of velcro just fitted, pin or tack the second part of velcro to match, then unfold and machine this second strip in place.

Fig. 6.2 Canvas worker's tool roll

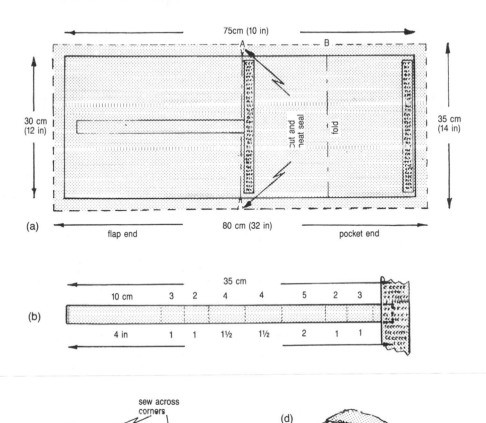

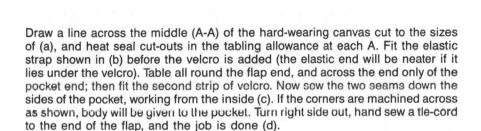

Draw a line across the middle (A-A) of the hard-wearing canvas cut to the sizes of (a), and heat seal cut-outs in the tabling allowance at each A. Fit the elastic strap shown in (b) before the velcro is added (the elastic end will be neater if it lies under the velcro). Table all round the flap end, and across the end only of the pocket end; then fit the second strip of velcro. Now sew the two seams down the sides of the pocket, working from the inside (c). If the corners are machined across as shown, body will be given to the pocket. Turn right side out, hand sew a tie-cord to the end of the flap, and the job is done (d).

Side seams Fold the pocket flap in half along B-B again, outsides touching this time, and so that its two velcro strips coincide but back to back; Fig. 6.2(c). Machine the two sides as round seams with a straight stitch; Fig. 4.3. To give some body to the pocket, machine across each bottom corner about 2–3 cm (1 in) in from its point (c). Turn the pocket right way out.

Lashing Hand sew the middle of about 90 cm (3 ft) of narrow cord to the centre of the outer edge of the flap tabling. This will tie round the roll when it is in use; Fig. 6.2(d).

Kit Bag

Design

As far as this book is concerned, the difference between a ditty bag and a kit bag is not only one of size, but it also takes account of the addition of a round panel at the latter's base.

Material Although my RAF kit bag was made of cotton, that was a long time ago, and I shall assume that synthetic cloth has been chosen – heavy 200–220 gm (6 oz) nylon, or possibly an acrylic (polyester would be rather hard). This will, of course, make it easier to sew, because there will be no need to double the tabling or seams. The diameter of the finished product will be exactly one third of the circumference (our old friend $2\pi\rho$ from school), so bear this in mind when you decide on sizes; Fig. 6.3 gives a suggestion for a bag 75 cm (30 in) tall and 30 cm (12 in) in diameter. I have allowed 4 cm (1½ in) for the drawstring tabling, and 1 cm (½ in) for both the side and base seams.

Manufacture

Much of the seaming will be similar to that of the ditty bag already described, but without the need to tuck the edges under. Heat seal both panels all round wherever there is no selvedge.

Tabling The drawstring tabling needs to be 4 cm (1½ in) minimum, and it should be tackled in the same way as that of the ditty bag – fold the corners over if the drawstring will be inside the tabling (Fig. 6.1); leave them square if you will be fitting eyelets; Figs. 6.1(f) and 6.3(b). Complete the tabling by machine with a straight stitch.

Centre seam Mate edge A_1 to A_2 in Fig. 6.3(b) with the inside out, and sew a straight stitch on the machine as a 1–2 cm (½ in) round seam (as shown in Fig. 4.3).

Circular base Turn up 1–2 cm (½ in) of the base panel all round, and crease it by rubbing down; Fig. 6.3(a). You will be working from the inside, so see that both outsides are facing inwards. Tack or pin the base panel in position and hand sew it (using the round seaming stitch of Fig. 3.4). You have to accept the small wrinkles caused by the circular shape – they won't show if you are working in nylon. Turn the bag the right way out.

Drawstring The drawstring is fitted in the same way as we saw for the ditty bag in Fig. 6.1(e) or (f). The job is then complete.

Fig. 6.3 Kit bag

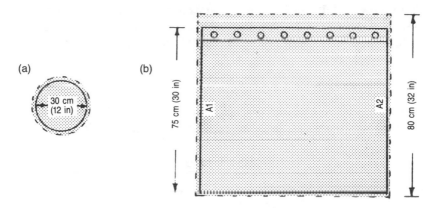

Table the top of the bag with the full tuck of Fig. 4.6(c), then mate edge A1 to A2 with the inside out, and machine together as a round seam (Fig. 4.3). You will need to cut away V-shapes from the base seam allowance if you are using a hard canvas which will not absorb wrinkles easily like nylon or acrylic. Punch in eight eyelets as shown (or any number divisible by four), to ensure that the drawstring runs on the outside across the back of the bag.

Sail Bag

Design

The difference between a sail bag and the kit bag we have just examined may be summarised as follows:

(a) Material;
(b) Diameter;
(c) Base panel.

Material These days, sail bags are nearly always made of 150–200 gm (4–6 oz) nylon, for it is soft and easily worked. Cotton and acrylic are not really contenders, the former because of mildew and the latter because of expense.

Diameter Sail bags need to be very roomy if their contents are not to be crushed. Ensure that the finished diameter is at least 50 cm (20 in) for all sails up to 20 m² (220 sq ft), if not 60 cm (24 in); go up in size as the sail gets bigger.

Base panel Above all, sail bags need to allow a good circulation of air, to prevent condensation building up when a damp sail is stowed away for a period of weeks. This is well achieved by making the base of nylon netting. If the mesh is too large, it will not respond to machine sewing very well, but its position at the base of the bag means that it will usually be easier to sew it by hand anyway.

Drawstring Plain cord tends to jam as a drawstring in soft nylon, so try using narrow tape of Terylene or nylon tape (government surplus parachute lines are good), or else soft nylon cord of about 5–6 cm (³⁄₁₆ – ¹⁄₄ in) diameter.

Manufacture

Make sail bags as you would kit bags, just described. The nylon netting base panel may need a little more care as you hand sew it.

Hatch Cover

Design

In this instance, I have assumed a square fo'cs'le hatch some 75 cm (2ft 6in) on each side, with enough height to allow a sensible 7–8 cm (3 in) skirt; Fig. 6.4. Some PVC-coated polyesters tend to shrink very slightly with age, so err on the loose side rather than the other way, if anything; but don't overdo it.

Material We discussed various materials for hatch covers in Chapter 2, and I shall assume that you will choose acrylic or PVC-coated nylon or polyester.

Manufacture

You will normally find that it is safer to mark your material for size on the hatch in question, rather than work from measurements. Use tailor's chalk, ordinary chalk or a pencil, whichever you find rubs out most easily. Press the cloth round the outside and rub your chalk along the outline, then mark the skirts required, allowing a tabling even if the fabric will heat seal; the edges will need strength for chafe, hooks or snaps of some kind.

Corners The figure shows two ways ot tackling the corners; (b) is slightly neater than (c), but also marginally less watertight. The corners in (c) are pinched together as shown, then sewn flat to one or other side of the skirt.

Fastenings If the cover needs to be secured, you may adopt one of the following methods; my vote goes for (b), (d) or (a) in that order.

(a) Shock cord drawstring (see Fig. 3.12);
(b) Velcro (see Fig. 3.13);
(c) Lift-the-dot fasteners (see Fig. 3.18);
(d) Press studs avoid the sharp projections of lift-the-dot fasteners (see Fig. 3.18);
(e) Turnbuttons (see Fig. 3.19).

Fig. 6.4 Hatch cover

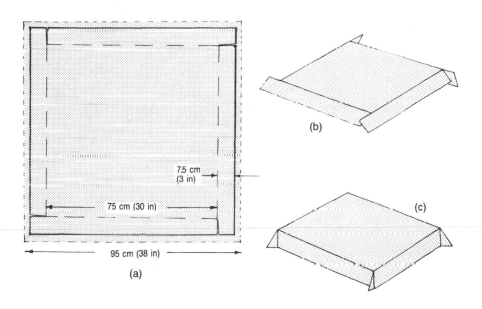

(b)

(c)

75 cm
(3 in)

75 cm (30 in)

95 cm (38 in)

(a)

When the canvas has been pressed on the hatch and chalked for size (a), the corner treatment must be considered. If you cut as in (b), the result will be neat but suspect with regard to waterproof qualities. To avoid cutting, pinch the corners as shown in (c) and sew the resulting pleat against the skirt.

Winch Cover

Design

An individual winch cover is more complicated than a simple boot added to a sail coat (see Fig. 7.2 in the next chapter). Even so, many winch covers merely sit loosely on the winch, waiting to be blown off; or else they have an inelegant lashing round the outside. I picked up this smart idea from Jim Grant of Sailrite Kits. The secret ingredient lies in the underskirt, which has a hem of shock cord to grip the narrow waist of the winch and hold the cover in place.

Material The outside material should match the rest of your covers, so I am again assuming either blue acrylic or else PVC-covered polyester or nylon. The petticoat or underskirt may be made of the same fabric, but you will produce a better result by using something less bulky such as a 150 gms (4–5 oz) nylon.

Measurements

Figure 6.5 shows a representative winch, with dimensions as given. The outer cover will be three times as long as the maximum winch diameter, plus an allowance of 1 cm (½ in) for the barrel seam. If the winch mounting block is a good deal larger in diameter than the winch itself, and you wish to cover it as well, you will have to allow extra cloth at the base. The cover's height will equal that of the winch plus a seam allowance at the top and a tabling allowance at the bottom (c).

The underskirt will be the same length (circumference) as the outer cover, but its height will only equal the distance from the winch top to the waist, plus allowances for a top seam and for a tabling to carry the shock cord which will hold it all in place (d).

The circular top of the cover will have a diameter equal to that of the winch, plus a 1 cm (½ in) allowance for the joining seam C in Fig. 6.5(b).

Manufacture

The cover can be made by taking the various steps in several different orders, but the following will be found convenient.

Tablings Machine the bottom tabling of the (larger) outer cover with a row of straight stitching along each side of the hem. Machine one row only along the inner edge of the shock cord tabling of the underskirt; if you fit a light line inside this tabling as you sew, you will save the bother of reeving a messenger later.

Barrel seams Fold each rectangular panel in half so that the shorter ends match AA to AA and BB to BB in Fig. 6.5(c) and (d), and with their insides facing outwards (e). Machine separately along those AA and BB edges as 1 cm (½ in) round seams, taking care not to sew across the ends of the smaller underskirt's tabling, in order to leave it free for passage of the shock cord later.

Top seam Crease the seam allowance into the circumference of the top panel with a rubbing iron (back of your knife or scissors), and fit all

Fig. 6.5 Winch cover

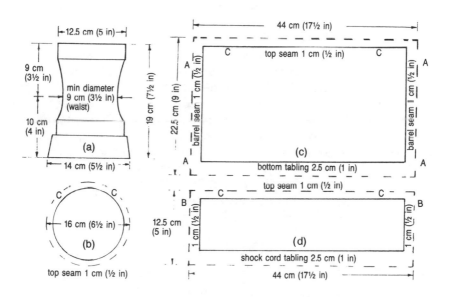

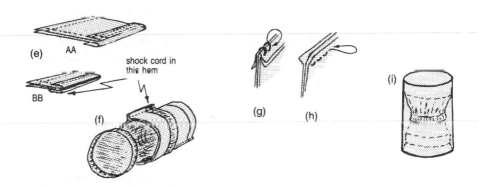

Table the lower hem of both outer cover and underskirt, leaving a free run for a shock cord drawstring in the latter, then work from the inside to form cylinders by using the round seam (don't block the run of the drawstring). Hand sew the circular panel to the top, noting my remarks in the main text about number of thicknesses of cloth; see (g) and (h). Fit shock cord into the tabling of the underskirt and adjust it so that it is about half the circumference of the narrow part of the winch (leaving a short length hanging free for later adjustment if it should prove too tight). Turn the work right side out and try it for size.

three pieces together along seams C as in Fig. 6.5(f) – still inside out. Hand sew the resulting circular seam. If you use the round seaming stitch as in Fig. 3.4, you will have six thicknesses to sew (g); if you stick them from side to side in the form of the close tacking stitch of Fig. 3.1(b), you will only have three thicknesses (h).

Shock cord   Now fit the shock cord into the tabling of the underskirt. If you did not sew in a messenger as you formed the tabling, use a tapestry needle or a large safety pin as a bodkin and reeve one now, then pull the shock cord through. The length of elastic cord should be roughly half the circumference of the winch barrel, but you will soon find what gives a snug fit at the narrowest part (if you are away from the boat, try it on a can or cup of the correct diameter); it is advisable to leave a short extra length of shock cord protruding so that adjustment may be made later. Sew both ends into the tabling to lock it all in place.

The cover is now finished. It only remains to turn it right side out and see what it looks like when fitted; Fig. 6.5(i).

Cockpit Pocket

Design

This pocket is designed to go on a bulkhead or cockpit side wall, to hold sheets, halyards, winch handles or the hundred and one other ropes, lines, levers and tools which can make life difficult or easy, according to how tidy and accessible they are.

I have suggested a finished size of 22–23 × 22–23 cm (9 × 9 in), with plenty of body in it to take a sheet or halyard but, of course, these measurements may be varied to suit the need; Fig. 6.6(d). The pocket consists of a back panel with a flap which forms the base (a), and a front panel with two side flaps (b). If you have a big enough piece of cloth, these two may be cut as one panel, being a single piece along side E in (a) and (b) – without the 1 cm (½ in) seam allowance, of course.

Manufacture

Straight stitching on the machine, with the pocket turned inside out, is the best in this instance. Before starting, punch the various drain and fixing holes as shown, finishing off with eyelets.

Tablings   A 2–3 cm (1 in) tabling is allowed as a hem at the top of both panels, the one to provide a secure fixing for the back, and the other to allow for shock cord closure at the front.

Seams   Machine the various seams together, as may be most convenient, preferably forming round seams as in Fig. 4.3, with the pocket inside out. Don't sew across the open ends of the front panel's shock cord tabling until the elastic has been fitted.

Finishing   Fit shock cord into the top tabling of the front panel, and sew it off so that there is tension on the cord. If you allow a short extra length to protrude, you will have some adjustment if you later find that you have made it too tight. The pocket is now turned right way out and screwed to the chosen bulkhead through a wooden batten which spreads the opening; Fig. 6.6 (c) and (d). It is a good idea to use large washers behind the fixing screws, so that the cloth does not get torn.

Fig. 6.6 Cockpit pocket

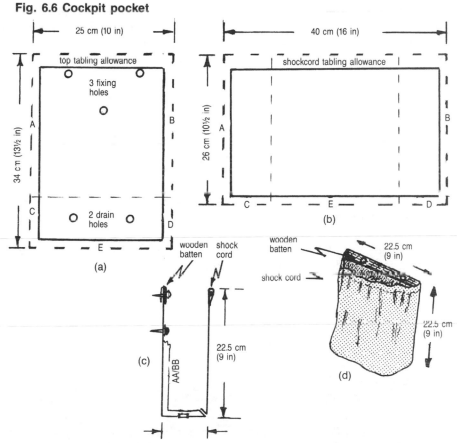

You will save yourself a bit of sewing if you cut the pocket panels (a) and (b) in one piece (joined along E). The back piece may not look essential, but it facilitates fixing the pocket to the bulkhead without too many gaps at the back. Let a short length of shock cord run out of the tabling, to allow a degree of adjustment until you have tried it for size.

Netting Shelf

Design

We have all suffered from lack of space in boats, whether it be the navigator seeking a readily accessible stowage for her parallel rule and tide tables, the skipper for the race instructions, or the foredeck gorilla for his girlie magazines. There is often unused space beneath the deckhead, and I certainly made use of this when I was racing a Dragon regularly.

Materials A fine mesh synthetic netting (the same as we decided on for the base of our sailbag) is easily installed, and allows its contents to be identified in situ. A length of shock cord is woven in and out along the front edge to hold the shelf tight enough to prevent spillage. The netting itself is fixed to the deckhead by means of staples if it is wood, battens if you have a head lining, or self-tapping screws for fibreglass.

Mast Coat

Design

Where a mast is stepped on the keelson, so that it passes through the deck, there must be an arrangement for keeping the deck watertight. If there is a slot for adjustment at the mast partners, this requirement cannot be met by a simple plastic or neoprene collar, so that a mast coat of waterproof canvas needs to be fitted. It is usually lashed tightly round the mast, and clamped at the deck under a wooden or metal ring; Fig. 6.7(d).

Material Traditionally mast coats were made of heavy cotton, proofed with various kinds of evil-smelling concoctions, often involving kutch, Stockholm tar, linseed oil and possibly varnish, egg whites, and anything else which the master thought would help keep the water out and preserve the canvas. Fortunately nowadays we have PVC-coated cloth, which may take the fun out of preparing a witches' brew of noxious ingredients, but makes life a lot easier – and less smelly.

Measurements

If the old coat has served well, and has enough shape left in it to act as a pattern, then use it as such. If you have to design from scratch, we are both indebted to Percy Blandford for a procedure which may have been used on the Ark, but was new to me when I read it in his book *Modern Sailmaking* (referenced at the end).

Measure the 'profile' of the desired finished coat (the 'end elevation' if you are a house architect; the 'side view' if you are a straightforward

Fig. 6.7 Mast coat

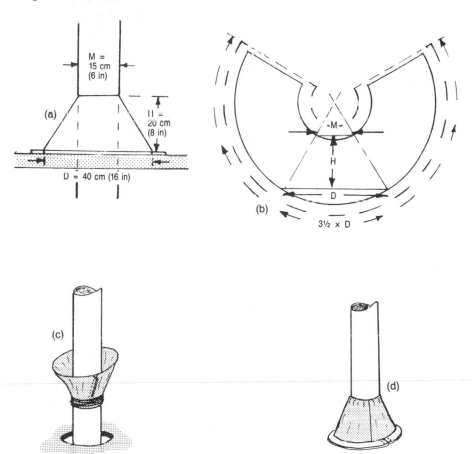

If you haven't got the old mast coat as a pattern, the secret is to establish the proper profile (a), and then to take care over cutting out the cloth (b). D is the diameter along the deck, M the diameter at the collar, and H the height of the collar above the deck. When drawing the paper pattern, first establish the shape M × H × D as shown in (b), then project the sloping slides until they meet. This is the centre of the two concentric arcs through the ends of M and D, to lengths of 3½ × M and D respectively (compare Fig. 7.7). Lash the coat underneath as shown in (c), then fold down to fit under the mast ring (d).

sort of chap like Percy) as in Fig. 6.7(a); M is the mast diameter, D the diameter at the deck, and H the height. Draw this full size on a paper pattern, and project the sloping sides to their intersection. Using this point as a centre, scribe an arc through the ends of D and with a length equal to $3^{1/2} \times$ D; then do the same for M. Add a small seam allowance at the ends, and allowances at the top for lashing, and at the bottom to go under the ring clamp; Fig. 6.7(b).

You are now ready to offer the paper pattern up to the mast and make any adjustments which may be necessary, before cutting out the cloth.

Manufacture

The mast ring will either be in two parts or, if it is a one-piece ring, already round the mast (if it isn't, you have problems!). Place the cloth upside down and inside out round the mast (c), and hand seam it with a flat-felled seam as in Fig. 3.6. Then lash the top securely at the correct point on the mast, so that the lashing will eventually be underneath. Now turn the coat down (right side out) and secure the base under the deck ring; Fig. 6.7(d).

Spinnaker Turtles

Design

How big should a spinnaker turtle be? This depends chiefly on the size of your spinnaker, but to a certain extent also on how you pack it. A turtle will, and should, compress the spinnaker rather more compactly than an ordinary sailbag. But you should allow yourself a little latitude, because the sail may sometimes be packed under less than ideal conditions (those who have done it lying on their ear, thrashing to windward in a heaving saloon, having just rounded the lee mark with only a short beat to a beam reach – and who hasn't? – may be permitted a wry smile at this understatement).

A broad rule of thumb, which I worked out some time ago and have found to be useful when there is no other yardstick, is to assume that one litre of turtle will hold about one square metre of sail (one cubic foot of turtle will hold approximately 350 sq ft of packed spinnaker). I have chosen three distinct types for your consideration: the pulpit turtle, the sailbag turtle, and the deck turtle. But you may launch a spinnaker from a cardboard box, or even from your arms in light weather.

Pulpit turtle

This is a launcher which I designed some twenty years ago for a three-ton cruising keelboat. It is shaped to fit into a small pulpit forward of the forestay, and can be adapted to suit most boats. The specification shown in Fig. 6.8 works out at about 30 litres (packing 30 m²) or one cu ft (packing 350 sq ft of spinnaker. (Thanks to W.G. Lucas for my original drawing).

Fig. 6.8 Spinnaker turtle – pulpit type

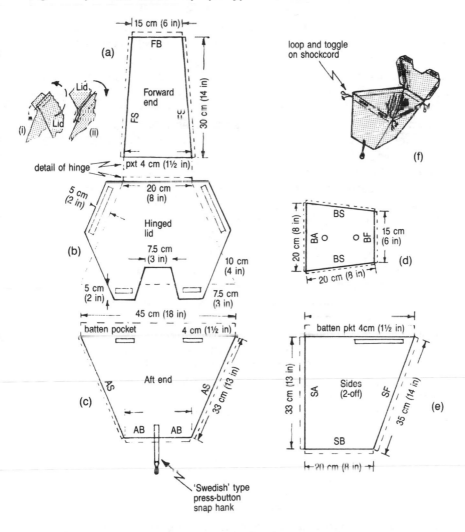

Cut out the various panels as shown, allowing seam allowances throughout. You can save some time by cutting two or more adjoining panels from a single piece of canvas (joined at the appropriate edges); if you decide to cut the top and forward end as one, you will need to make a special pocket for the batten. Sew velcro to the body of the turtle **before** you form the batten tablings, so as not to sew through the pockets; leave fitting the matching parts until you are nearly finished (this will ensure a good fit, and enable some extra bulk to be given to the turtle if necessary). Don't forget the tie-down snap hank, or you may lose the whole thing overboard the first time you use it!

Note that the two aft corners and the centre portion of the lid are cut away to accommodate the clews and the head.

Material   We always used to make this turtle in PVC-coated cloth, but most other kinds of marine canvas would work as well. Two drain holes are required in the base (as in every turtle); plus suitable fixing points (a couple of shock cord loops with toggles for fastening round the pulpit legs, and a Swedish snap hank on a short line at the base to stop the whole contraption from being hoisted aloft or lost overboard); also some strategically placed velcro strips to keep the lid shut until the halyard pulls it open; and finally you will need some strips of wood or ABS battening to hold the square opening in shape.

Eyelets   Punch the eyelets into the base while you can get at it easily (there will be reasonable access even when the job is complete, so don't worry if you forget).

Hinge   The first joining seam to be sewn should be the hinge; this should be done before the batten pockets are sewn. Lie the Lid and the Forward End on top of each other, with their outsides touching and their hinge lines matching; machine the two together as a flat seam with a straight stitch; detail in Fig. 6.8(a) (i). The wide part of the hinge flap should now be folded flat against the inside surface of the Forward End and machined along its outer edge to form a pocket, as shown in (a) (ii).

Batten pockets   Before sewing down the batten pockets, machine one part of each velcro pairing to the body of the turtle, taking care to position each one so that a little slack can be allowed to the lid flaps in case the spinnaker bulges a bit. First join the hinge as just described, then machine the batten pockets in the wide part of the Forward and Aft Ends, and the two Sides, as shown in Fig. 6.8(a), (c) and (e); leave them open to accept the battens later.

Seams   The remaining seams are then machined as round seams; Fig. 4.3, with the turtle inside out; SA (Side, Aft end) joins AS (Aft end, Side); SF (Side, Forward end) joins FS (Forward end, Side); SB (Side, Base) joins BS (Base, Side); AB (Aft end, Base) joins BA (Base, Aft end); and FB (Forward end, Base) joins BF (Base, Forward end).

Attachments   The matching parts of the four velcro strips already sewn are now positioned on the lid flaps and machined in place, allowing some slack for a bulging lid. Loops and toggles are fitted where they can embrace the pulpit legs. A tie-down strop is added so it can hank to the genoa tack fitting, or go round a mooring bollard, or hook to some other suitable point.

Up spinnaker!

Sailbag turtle

A round spinnaker bag makes a useful launcher, in that it may be used forward of the forestay in the same manner as the pulpit turtle just described; it may also be clipped to the lee guardrail or shrouds or, indeed, anywhere on the foredeck; in light weather it may be held in the arms. The one illustrated in Fig. 6.9 has a volume of 55 litres (packing 55 m²) or 1.7 cu ft (packing 600 sq ft). You may adjust its capacity before you start making it, by varying its height – or its diameter, for that matter, though this latter will also entail altering the circumference panel's length as well as its height. When you are working out the dimensions you need, for our purposes, volume may be taken as 3 × diameter × height.

An alternative is to get an existing sailbag of convenient diameter and put the spinnaker into it; press it down and measure the height required. Or you can ensure that the one you are making is slightly too tall, and cut it down before finishing the top tabling.

Material   Fairly heavy nylon is almost as good as any for this turtle; polyester or PVC-coated cloth will also do, but nylon folds into a smaller space when not in use. This is basically a sailbag with a lid, plus a couple of tie-downs and, if you want the de luxe version, a hoop to hold it open.

Sizes   Suggested sizes are shown in Fig. 6.9. As I say, these particular measurements will produce a volume to pack a spinnaker of 55 m² (600 sq ft); if you want more or less, get your calculator out.

The lid   The round lid drawn in (a) is reached by taking the circumference of the bag itself (in this case, 135 cm (54 in); then determining the outer circumference of the lid tabling as drawn to scale, to provide a 7.5 cm (3 in) rim with a 2.5 cm (1 in) tabling, giving a total of 195 cm (78 in). Subtract one from the other to show how much has to be cut out of the outer circle, so that it will fold down to match the bag circumference – in this case, 60 cm (24 in) must be taken out in segments. This chops neatly into eight 3 in segments (you wouldn't expect me to make my example difficult, would you?), with the result you see; if you are working in centimetres, you could either take out six segments of 10 cm, or else ten segments of 6 cm. Note that the sides of the flaps have to be parallel if the rim is to hang at right angles. You could try not cutting at all, but there would be a lot of crimping and bunching at the edge of the rim, even though you are using nylon.

Seaming   Join the lid cut-outs together, and then fold over the tabling to take a length of shock cord. The rest of the bag is put together like a sailbag except that, after the rectangular panel has been seamed into a cylinder, an ABS or cane ring is sewn into its tabling – usually a hand job. Sew one side of the lid to the bag proper for about 15 cm (6 in) of its circumference, to act as a hinge.

Attachments Sew shock cord into the lid rim for a snug fit, and add one or more loop and toggle fixings, or else a snap hook or two. Punch a couple of drain eyelets into the base, and the turtle is ready; Fig. 6.9(e).

Fig. 6.9 Spinnaker turtle – bag type

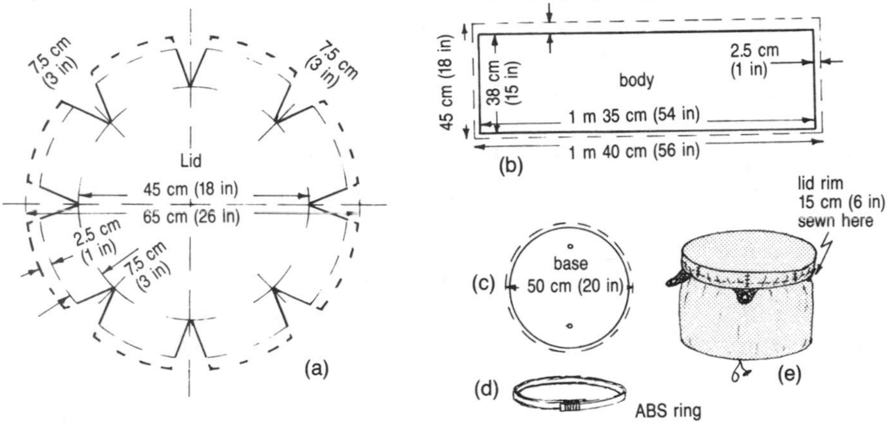

If hoisting from the lee rail is your bag, then this is the bag for you. I have divided the skirt on the lid into eight sections, but use however many makes for easy mathematics (ten here, if you are dealing in metrics). The sides of the segments need to be parallel if the outer perimeter is to be the same length as the inner (i.e. the skirt will then hang at right angles). You will see that I have included an ABS ring to hold the circular top open.

Deck turtle

I used to have something rather like this turtle, flat on the foredeck of my Dragon immediately in front of the forestay (it needs a fair amount of open space). The one in Fig. 6.10 contains about 25 litres (packing 25 m²) or ³/₄ cu ft (packing 275 sq ft).

Material The flat base of this turtle is made of plywood; to it is stitched, glued, screwed or battened a single panel of PVC-coated cloth. The turtle is only open at its aft end, and this is restricted by tight-fitting shock cord. There are the usual drain holes and tie-downs.

Plywood base Cut the plywood to size and give it two or three coats of varnish. There is a V-shaped cut-out at the centre of the aft edge, designed to fit either side of the forestay, but this may not be right for your boat; and there are drain holes and hand-holds on either side; see Fig. 6.10(a).

Top panel Allow some 10 per cent extra cloth at either side, plus a radius at the forward and aft ends, to give the turtle some body; add

4 cm (1½ in) for a shock cord tabling aft, and a similar allowance on the other three sides for fixing under the edges of the board. Figure 6.10(b) shows this panel with a dot-dash outline of the plywood base underneath it.

Assembly   Sew the tabling round the loose shock cord. Fix the panel to the plywood base, forward and at each side (glue will probably eventually come unstuck, so it may be best to drill a few holes in the board and then sew the cloth to it; you can drill the drain holes at the same time). Make the shock cord fast at one end, and tighten it fairly hard before making fast at the other end.

The bag is now ready for use; Fig. 6.10(c).

Fig. 6.10 Spinnaker turtle – deck type

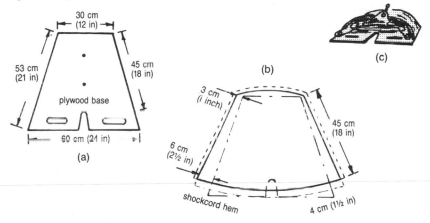

The biggest spinnaker which can be pulled easily out of a turtle this shape is some 50 m² (500–600 sq ft). The trickiest part is to ensure that the PVC (or whatever) is fastened properly to the plywood.

Wind Scoop

Design

A wind scoop, sometimes known as a galley sail or a wind catcher, makes a big difference to life below decks in the tropics. There are de luxe models which will catch the wind whatever its direction, and also keep out the rain (see Jim Grant's book among the References), but I am only including here a simple design which you can run up quickly.

I first saw this suggested in 1985, when Lin and Larry Pardey wrote about it in *Practical Boat Owner*. In tideless conditions, a yacht will usually lie head to any wind there is. The scoop will then fit over the forehatch, facing forward, and be tied off either side (perhaps to the shrouds) and aft to the mast; Fig. 6.11(c).

Material   As this is essentially a fair weather scoop, the material recommended by the Pardeys is spinnaker nylon, and I can have no argument with this. Decide on the height you want (the Pardeys suggest 1 m 20 cm (4 ft) as against the 1m 50 cm (5 ft) which I have given), then draw it full size on your length of nylon, allowing a slight 'fullness' to give the scoop some body; Fig. 6.11(a). Each base will need to run along one side of the hatch and half way across one of the other sides. Tack the two pieces together down the spine, and offer it to the hatch. You will now find why I have been slightly generous with my height; you may need to throw more curve into the centre seam, or even to put some into each 'luff', in order to get it sitting with a nice fullness. This would entail reducing the height to get the extra 'flow'.

Fig. 6.11 Wind scoop

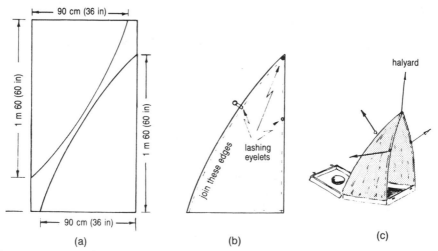

(a)   (b)   (c)

The nylon is cut with a hot knife, allowing a convex curve to the spine (a). The tablings shown in (b) should have the full tuck of Fig. 4.6 (c), to give some added strength to the eyelets. The centre seam along the spine will be stronger if the flat-felled seam of Fig. 4.5 is used, otherwise use the round seam of Fig. 4.3(b) backed with a length of tape.

Manufacture

Having finalised the sizes (b), join the two cloths along the centre with a round seam (inside out), and run a tabling round the other two edges – tucked right under as Fig. 4.6(c) to give three thicknesses of cloth for eyelets or lashing attachments (you could add tape at the bottom, if it looks particularly fragile).

Fittings Arrange to fit the scoop onto the hatch with one of the attachments suggested in Chapter 3; punch in a halyard eyelet at the head but not yet on the 'luffs'. Try it out on the hatch, and then decide where to fit the necessary lashings; you will probably need a tab hank on the spine to tie away behind the scoop. Remember that this wind catcher may need to be fitted athwartships or even facing aft one day, so see that all lashings will do double duty.

Windows

Design and manufacture

If you decide that you would like to put a window into a cockpit awning, a sail, a windbreak or a tent, don't rush into it by immediately cutting the opening you want. The correct way is to mark where the window should lie, cut the sheet of clear PVC to size, and sew it to the *uncut* canvas; Fig. 6.12(a) (over) shows Plastipane being sewn across the seam of an awning.

Turn the whole thing over and *now* cut out the canvas (if you do it any earlier, you will have difficulty keeping distortion away as you sew the window). Figure 6.12(b) shows a hot knife working against a flexible metal scraper, to seal as you cut. Sew a second row of stitching round close to the first, and the job is done (c).

If you want the window to look smart, you can machine a tape round the raw edge of Plastipane, but this is an unessential refinement.

Guardrail Spray Dodgers

Design

The guardrail spray dodger is one of the easiest of canvas jobs, provided you get the basic measurements correct. It is a straightforward panel which requires no shaping; the only points worth noting being the method of attachment, and the need to leave a narrow gap each end for tension, and a slightly larger one at the bottom for the passage of sheets and mooring lines; Fig. 6.13 (over).

Material I keep banging on about acrylic or PVC-covered cloth, but there really is no sensible alternative.

Fig. 6.12 Windows

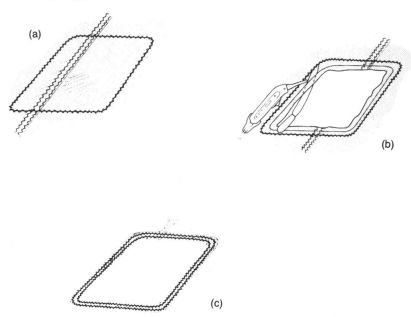

I have shown a seam running across the proposed window in (a), purely to make the drawings clearer. After the window material has been cut to size and sewn to the uncut spread of canvas, turn the job over and cut the unwanted cloth away, preferably with a hot (b). Sew down the reverse side and turn it back again for admiration (c).

Fig. 6.13 Guardrail spray dodgers

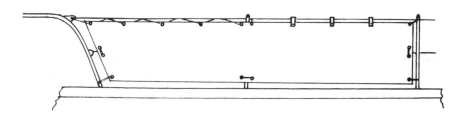

Ensure that your panels are a little smaller than the space you want to fill, so that the dodgers will be held in tension. Leave a gap at the bottom, for the easier run of sheets and mooring lines.

Manufacture

Measure the guardrail and see that the finished dodger will be short enough at each end to permit some tension on the lashings. I have shown both a continuous lacing and tab hanks in my drawing. As a dodger is not usually taken off frequently, we may accept the tedious nature of continuous lacing in order to achieve the benefit of the better security which it offers. If you are going to remove part of it regularly (to break the guardrail for a gangway, perhaps), then you may prefer the quicker press studs or tab fasteners which I showed at Fig. 3.17. In any event, make sure that you have a wide tabling as a form of reinforcement.

Name

Painting a name on these dodgers is made easier if you use masking tape as a guideline (both paint and masking tape adhere better to PVC-coated cloth rather than acrylic). Or you may buy stick-on letters from your sailmaker, and then machine them down as well; use of a silicone release agent in the form of a lubricant spray will help prevent the machine needle from sticking with the adhesive.

Bunk Leecloths

Design and manufacture

Another simple task with no shaping needed, leecloths may be made of virtually any canvas short of spinnaker nylon, which would be too weak. You may find that 150 gm/m^2 (4 oz/yd^2 or 3½ oz/US) polyester is as good as any.

Fig. 6.14 Bunk leecloths

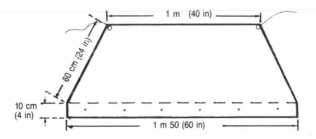

A scrap piece of sailcloth is as good as anything for this easy task. The distance along the top needs to be less than the distance separating the hooks in the deckhead, so that the leecloth is held in tension fore and aft as well as up and down.

About the only consideration involved is the need to ensure that the attachment points in the deckhead are spaced more widely apart than the lashings in the top corners of the leecloth. This will ensure that there is a certain tension to spread the leecloth; Fig. 6.14.

Fender Covers

Design

Plastic fenders are so cheap and efficient that I don't propose to offer any suggestions for making a fender from filled canvas – it would be a waste of your time and mine. But scooter tyres or those from a garden trolley make excellent permanent dockside fenders, or even for carrying aboard a large vessel. Their main drawbacks are indifferent looks, and the scuff marks they cause as rubber is smeared across white topsides. So let's have a look at how to cover them; Fig. 6.15.

Fig. 6.15 Fender cover

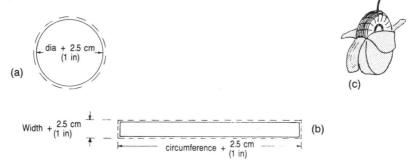

Work this one inside out until you can only just get the tyre into the partly sewn cover (c). You now have to finish from the outside as neatly as you can.

Material   Two circles of polyester, preferably coated with PVC, equal to the size of the tyre plus a seam allowance for the join, will form the two sides (a). A strip of the same material (b) will join these two together.

Manufacture

Join the three pieces inside out, with the round seaming stitch of Fig. 3.4, half-way round the two circumferences. Turn the job the right way out and try the tyre for size. If it fits, turn it inside out again and finish one of the circles. A hanging cord is inserted through the tyre, with a stopper of some sort inside it, and then the tyre is refitted. The final seam has to be hand sewn from the outside.

Cook's Harness

Design and manufacture

Some form of adjustable restraining strap round the small of the back can make all the difference to cooking aboard a boat in a lumpy seaway. The sizes shown in Fig. 6.16 are reasonable for most circumstances, but it would be as well to test them. Take a tape measure to your galley, decide where the anchoring eyebolts will be sited, and then think about strap length. Allow for snap hooks of some sort at each end – one shackled and the other on a lanyard for adjustment.

The strap itself is 90 cm (3 ft) of 7–8 cms (3 in) webbing cut with a hot knife. Hand sew D-rings at each end and the job is complete, apart from attaching the hooks.

Fig. 6.16 Cook's harness

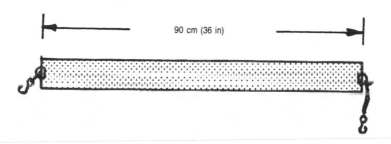

A wide webbing is more comfortable than a narrow one. Note the lashing at one end for adjustment.

Document Pouch

Design

It's no good owning a boat which looks smart with fancy covers, if you are for ever mislaying the ship's papers when abroad; you'll end up by having your pride and joy impounded, unless you make one of these pouches. It is large enough to take an A.4 document unfolded, with a zip closure which can be padlocked to an eyelet if necessary. It will thus keep your papers safe when you need to take them from their files and, being waterproof, will also see that they stay clean and dry; Fig. 6.17.

Materials You need no more than 30–35 cms (about 1ft) of PVC-coated fabric from a 1 metre (or 3 ft) wide roll; plus a 30 cm (12 in) closed end zipper; and an eyelet (e).

Fig. 6.17 Document pouch

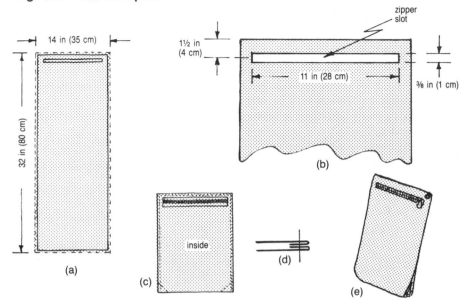

The sizes shown in (a) will comfortably take a sheet of A4 paper without folding. The slot (b) should be checked for size and clearance against the zipper to be used before it is cut. Machine the zipper in place before the pouch is folded and sewn (c). The end is closed from the outside, by tucking the cloths under as in (d).

Manufacture

Fit the zipper first. Cut a slot 1 cm (³/₈ in) wide, and 28 cm (11 in) long, along one of the shorter sides, with its centreline 4 cm (1½ in) from the edge of the canvas. Check that this covers both ends of your zipper, yet leaves the teeth nicely exposed all along each side. Fix the closed zipper in place with pins, then machine two rows of straight stitching down each side of the zip and across its ends (b). Reinforce the ends with leather or vinyl patches as shown in Fig. 3.14(d).

Fold the panel in half, inside out (c), and straight stitch the two side seams ½ cm (¼ in) inside the edge (c). Run a row across each bottom corner to give the pouch some bulk (as shown in Fig. 6.2).

Turn the work right side out, then tuck in ½ cm (¼ in) of each raw edge of the open end, and machine together (d), to close the whole pouch. Punch an eyelet into the top corner next to the slider when it is closed, and you can now lock it; Fig. 6.17(e).

Garden Weedsheet

We now turn to slightly more mundane matters, such as gardening. This proposal is a simple square of reinforced polyethelene cloth, with a rope handle at each corner. When you are condemned to weeding, drag it round after you and, when the groundsel, docks, dandelions and dead flowers need carting away to the compost heap, gather all four corners together and carry them off.

Fig. 6.18 Garden weedsheet

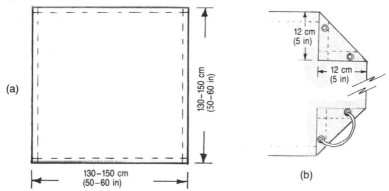

Having formed the simple tabling according to Fig. 4.6(a), fold the corners as in (b) here, in order to give some strength to this quickie.

Manufacture

Cut a square of polyethelene approximately to the sizes shown in Fig. 6.18(a), and run a tabling round all four sides. Sew down each corner as in the detail at (b), and punch in a couple of eyelets; fit a short length of rope as a handle, knotting the ends. All is now done (would that the weeding were as easy).

Garden Tidy Bag

This bag is a slightly more sophisticated version of the Garden Weedsheet; it is based on the sort of bag you may see being trundled round in a supermarket trolley. Again, it is made of reinforced polyethelene; Fig. 6.19.

Fig. 6.19 Garden tidy bag

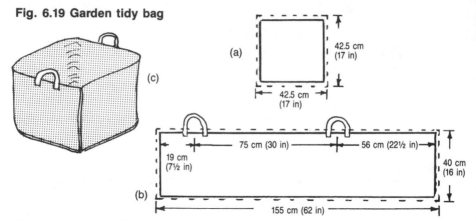

The handles look offset in (b), but they will be opposite one another provided the joining seam runs down to one corner of the base, if I have done my sums correctly.

Manufacture

Cut out the panels as shown in (a) and (b). I have allowed 2.5 cm (1 in) all round for secure seams and tabling, as this bag will be subject to some rough use. Run a tabling along the top edge of the larger piece (b). Working from the inside, join the two shorter ends of the large panel with the round seam of Fig. 4.3 then, starting with this join at one corner, add the base panel, again with the round seam. Turn the bag the right way out.

Handles may either be of tape sewn directly to the tabling, or else short lengths of rope run through eyelets as for the weedsheet shown in Fig. 6.18(b); they should be fitted either side of the centres as measured in Fig. 6.19(b) – provided the vertical joining seam runs down to one corner of the base panel.

All this talk of gardening makes me nervous. Let's get back to boats....

7 Advanced Work

The products tackled in this chapter are not necessarily any more difficult to make than those in Chapter 6 — they just take a bit longer. But there is much satisfaction to be gained (as well as money to be saved) by completing a major project for oneself. So let's get down to one or two of them, and you'll quickly find that there are no hidden terrors.

Wheel Cover

Design

I originally put this one into the previous chapter, because it is a fairly small job, and soon completed if there are no complications. But then I thought of the many boats which have rather more than the simple wheel and binnacle which I have assumed; apart from a grabrail, there may be engine controls, wind instruments, or automatic steering among other protuberances. So I added a few remarks on how to accommodate them, and switched it to this chapter, where it may start us off lightly.

As I have already suggested, many wheel/binnacle combinations also have a grabrail fitted permanently in front of, and higher than, the compass. If yours is one of these, the cover I suggest at Fig. 7.1 is easily modified by cutting a slit and adding a cap over the grabrail (see the treatment of a windshield in the boat cover dealt with in Fig. 7.6). I detail here only the simpler version, which will reveal the main features; you will have to alter my sizes to suit your own boat, and it is no great problem to cap a grabrail. Instrument consoles and engine controls may be another thing, depending where they occur. You should, however, be able to tackle them when you have cut your teeth on some simpler jobs; see the halyard winch boot illustrated at Fig. 7.2(d), and the boat cover boots in Fig. 7.5.

Material You will probably want to keep all your covers in one material, for appearance's sake if for no other reason; there is not much to challenge blue acrylic or PVC-coated cloth of some kind.

Fig. 7.1 Wheel and binnacle cover

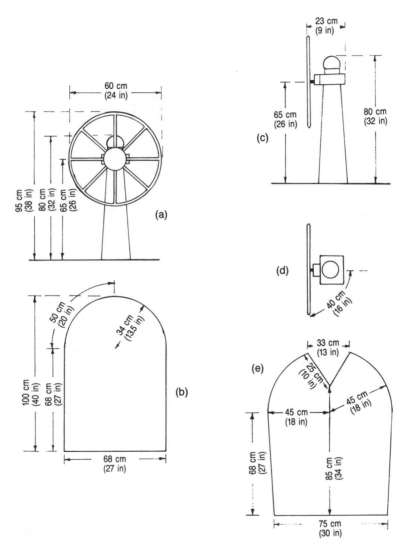

The slightly larger shaped panel of (e), must have a distance round its finished semi-circular top equal to the same part of the smaller flat panel shown in (b), even though the former starts with a larger radius. The cut-out must be calculated to achieve this as well as the necessary shaping (I have allowed a small seam allowance). A refinement is to add sand in small polythene bags sewn into the bottom tabling, to keep the cover weighed down to the cockpit floor.

Measurements   Take the principal measurements shown in Fig. 7.1 (a), (c) and (d), then draw to scale the two panels at (b) and (e). The width of the upper part of the panel at (e) must be equal to the curved distance from either side of the wheel, forward round the binnacle. This results in a 30 per cent greater radius for the semi-circle at its top, yet this circumference must be mated with the plain panel at (b). The V-shaped cut-out must therefore be tailored not only to provide the shape which accommodates the bulge of the compass but, at the same time, must remove the correct amount of circumference so that the two curved distances match.

Manufacture

As this is an awkward shape, I have allowed $2\frac{1}{2}$ cm (a full inch) for each seam; this will provide a small latitude in fitting; double it if you are in doubt. Join the two short arms of the V-shaped cut-out of Fig. 7.1(e) in a flat seam (Fig. 4.4), and then match the shaped result to the flat panel of Fig. 7.1(b), inside out. Tack or staple the two halves together, turn the result right way out and offer it up to the wheel, making any adjustments required.

The bottom of the cover will need to be shortened at the cockpit grating, for I have allowed a wide tabling; turn it under itself for added durability. Mark this at fitting time, for trimming if necessary.

The assembly is now ready to have its tabling machined with a straight stitch (Fig. 4.6) and then the two halves joined permanently in a round seam; Fig. 4.3. A refinement is to glue a short length of velcro to the top of the wheel in the fore and aft position, with a matching strip on the inside of the cover to hold it in place. The wheel velcro also acts as a dead centre indicator when sailing.

Sail Cover

Design

A sail cover can pay for itself quite quickly if the boat frequents tropical waters. The ultraviolet rays of the sun will degrade polyester sailcloth to the point where it will tear like paper if it is subjected to continued sunlight day in and day out for a year or so; even if the sails are inhibited, the thread used in their making is too fine for 100 per cent inhibition, and this will eventually weaken.

To avoid condensation, air must be able to circulate underneath a sail cover. This means that either the material from which the cover is made should be porous, or else the design of the cover should be such as to allow air movement inside.

Of the two, the second is the better solution, because porous cloth will allow rain as well as air to penetrate to the sails, unless it has been treated by a dry chemical process; even then, dirt in the weave will encourage wicking, which is the seepage of humidity through the cloth by means of soaking into the dirt particles.

Material   We are down to acrylic and PVC again. Being of a matt finish, acrylic somehow looks better; it certainly hangs well, and it is resistant to UV attack. But thousands of good sail covers are made of PVC-coated cloth, which has the advantage that it is cheaper than acrylic.

A sail cover is best made in two matching halves, with a seam along the top. The two halves should hang slackly down each side of the boom, and be joined underneath it loosely enough to allow air to circulate.

The forward end is carried upwards as it nears the mast, where the average sail builds up on its track when furled; the neck of the cover reaches higher than the head of the sail. The whole of the front of the cover reaches forward of the mast, with the top being lashed above the headboard, and the rest of it secured by some sort of lacing; see Fig. 7.2.

The collars must fit snugly round the mast and boom, beyond the sail in both cases. The nature of a mainsail stow means that the bulk of the sail lies well forward, and there will be an inward curve just behind the mast, with the cover tapering rapidly towards the clew.

The flaps at the front should overlap, with a lacing running slightly off centre as in (c), so I have allowed an extra 10 cm (4 in), forward of the distance which equals half the girth at the four mast measuring stations (the diagonal measurement down to the tack area is not essential, but it is a sensible check distance). See below under *Mast lashing*.

The seam allowance along the spine of the cover should be small, in order that it should remain unobtrusive. Tablings, on the other hand, need to be wide, so that not only is there strength, but also plenty of room for the eyelets, hooks and/or loops which will be required.

Measurements   If you are setting about replacing an existing cover which fits but is worn out, use the old one as a pattern, to the point where you should carefully unpick it if necessary, or cut it along its seams. If you are starting from scratch, however, take the measurements shown in Fig. 7.2(a) as a minimum; the ovals show which are girths, and I have given some suggested sizes so that they may be related to the pattern in Fig. 7.2(b).

Manufacture

Assuming that the sail coat will not need to go further up the mast than the width of the cloth available, the cover may be cut in two identical pieces; if additional height is required, an extra piece will need to be sewn to the top. Acrylic and PVC usually come in two widths: 1 m (40 in) and 1.5 m (60 in); in addition, some of the heavier PVC-coated polyesters (500–600 gm or 15–20 oz) can be obtained as wide as 2.5m (100 in). So it is worth looking around if your cover needs to be over a metre high.

The two sides being identical, one drawing will cater for them both. Draw it to scale and then fit it onto the width of the cloth at your disposal; it should be possible to fit the two cloths as shown in (b). If extra pieces are needed to make the height, their size and shape will be revealed as you fit the profile onto the scaled cloth width. These pieces can sometimes be fitted into the pattern by juggling the positions of the main panels, but you will only save a hand's span of canvas, so you might as well give them their own short strip.

When you start with the scissors, it is important to cut one panel only. This is because the final cover will be symmetrical, and this is best achieved by using the first panel as a pattern for the second. Similarly, if you need the small extra section to make the collar high enough up the mast, cut it generously large and stitch it (with the flat felled seam of Fig. 4.5) to the main panel *before* finalising the outline of the upper body; this will ensure a smooth sweep to the cover.

When you have got one panel right, draw its outline on the cloth in order to make the second, taking care to see that both inside surfaces are touching when the cloths are superimposed. While this is being marked, take the opportunity to put match marks down the two spines for use later when seaming them together.

Seaming The spine seam will need an allowance of 2 cm (¾ in) each side, despite the fact that you want to keep it small; this is because you will be using the flat felled seam of Fig. 4.5 due to its superior watertight qualities. Before sewing this seam, however, it is advisable to staple the panels together along the spine and offer them up to the sail in its normal furled position on the boom – with stapler to hand so that you can make any adjustments. If the curve of the spine is too sharp for the flat felled seam, use the round seam and sew a tape or webbing along it as in Fig. 4.3(b), adding a sealer such as Duroseam® or Seamkote®

Winch boot If a halyard winch needs to be accommodated, mark the spot at this time, cut a suitable hole and fit a small boot fashioned along the lines of the outer cover of Fig. 6.5 – made, as usual, inside out, and substituting a seam allowance for the tabling around the base; Fig. 7.2(d).

Mast lashing The easiest way to form the full mast collar, and front lacing, is to allow the front flap of each side panel to wrap round the forward side of the mast and overlap the half-way point by about half a

Fig. 7.2 Sail cover

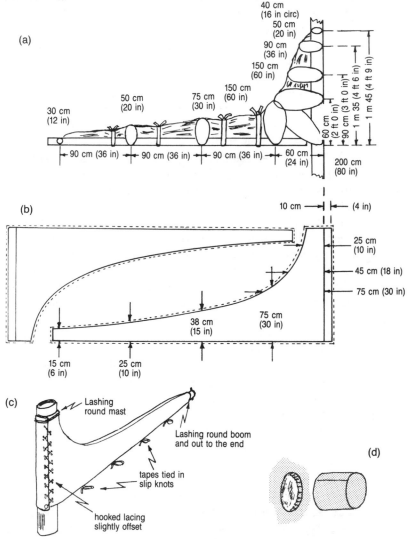

The boom length I have shown in (a) divides neatly into four stations; you will probably not be so lucky, and will have to deal in fractions. Whatever happens, you can't take too many measurements. Don't pull the tape too tight when going round the furled sail, if you have made a neat stow – it won't always be like that. Note that each side panel in (b) measures at each station half the corresponding circumference from (a), plus the tabling and mast flap allowance. The drawing at (d) is a small boot, added to fit over a mast winch.

mast width. One flap then goes under the other, and both are laced together; see Fig. 7.2(c). A short lashing is sewn to the side of the upper corner of the outside flap and passed round the mast a couple of times, before being tied off; a longer one is used to lash through hooks or eyelets on the under flap, along the lines of Figs. 3.15 or 3.16.

Boom lashing There should be a single short lashing at the outer end of the cover to tie round the boom and through the opposite corner of the cover, before being pulled to a convenient eye at the end of the boom. There are almost as many ways of lacing a sail cover underneath a boom as there are sailmakers, ranging from a zipper (too airtight), through shock cord lacing with opposing hooks (quick, but the hooks can scratch the boom if they are inside the cover, or catch on stray lines or clothing if they are outside), or a continuous lacing through alternate eyelets (tedious), to press fasteners of one kind or another (they can corrode). I would like to put in a word for a simple system of tapes on each side, which are tied together in a bow – this quick and corrosion-free idea is used by W.G. Lucas & Son; an extension of the same system is achieved by shock cord loops and mating toggles.

Boat Cover

Design

When designing a boat cover, you should establish whether you are going to use a ridge pole (or the main boom, if the boat is a sailing yacht with the spars left in); this increases efficiency by promoting air circulation, and it also reduces the risk of water collecting in pools, because steep run-offs are provided. Ridge poles usually run the length of the boat (perhaps resting on pulpit and pushpit), but they can run athwartships, or else be used vertically like a tent pole.

You should decide at this stage how you are going to fasten the cover. If it is an extended cockpit cover on a motor cruiser, you may prefer some kind of positive metal fitting which fastens to studs on the hull superstructure (cockpit coaming and cabin top). If you are covering a small dinghy which has a stout fender, you could adopt a drawstring which tightens round the hull and under the fender. A five-ton keelboat in a cradle ashore may need lines passed under the hull; the same boat afloat may have to resort to the toe-rail or fairleads (if there are not enough strategically placed strongpoints, you might have to use weighted bags at certain places).

Material Cotton is used quite a lot for overall boat covers, despite the fact that it is liable to mildew if not looked after properly. This is because a fairly slack weave of natural fibres will breathe when dry, but the fibres swell when wet and close the weave; cotton is also cheaper than most man-made cloth, which can be quite a factor where a big cover is involved.

Measurement   Having settled on the broad principles of your design, you now have to measure up. Only those covers for dinghies of a standard class can be produced in series to a standard pattern; all others of any size have to be custom made. Fit your ridge pole if applicable and measure the overall length of cover you will need, allowing 15 cm (6 in) over and above any overhang you propose (at each end). Now establish the general shape by measuring the vessel's beam (over the ridge pole), plus overhangs, plus 15 cm (6 in) each side. Start at the transom, and make your second station forward of that by the width of the cloth you will be using, less the stern overhang and less the 15 cm (6 in) tabling allowance; further stations will be at cloth width intervals from there forwards; Fig. 7.3.

Fig. 7.3 Boat cover – measuring

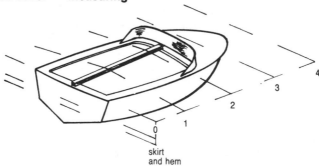

Stations are taken at cloth width intervals, after deducting the skirt and tabling allowance from the first width at the stern. Measure over any ridge pole.

Manufacture

Make a scale drawing of your measurements, and you are ready to start cutting rag; Fig. 7.4. You will start by making one large sheet, big enough to spread across the whole area to be covered, with its overhangs or skirts plus a hem or tabling allowance; ours will be made up of lengths of cloth running athwartships. Cut your strips as measured and mark their mid-length points, then join them to one another using the flat felled seam of Fig. 4.5, so that the mid-length marks coincide.

Shape is given to the flat sheet by mitre-cutting into the three corners (two at the transom and one at the bow), and allowing for the overhang plus a good tabling allowance; triangular pieces are cut out and the bare edges joined to make the shaped corner. Minor adjustments may be made by inserting darts, much as a dressmaker inserts gussets. These should be tried by pinching first and then either marking with a pencil or chalk, or else pinning. Fold over without cutting the cloth if the dart is small enough.

Fig. 7.4 Boat cover – main panel

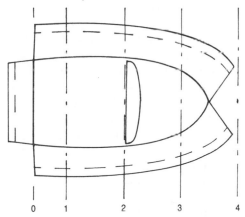

Corner cut-outs in excess of 90 degrees will pull in towards the hull when sewn together, so that a lacing of some sort will be required at the bow; see Figs. 3.15 and 3.16.

Boots   Major breaks in the surface may be accommodated by cutting into the cover and building up a new piece to fit, much as we saw for the boot fashioned for a winch under a sail coat; Fig. 7.2(d). This holds good for windshields, horns, small flagstaffs or radomes. First mark the underside of the cover with a plan view of the object to be accommodated, and then cut away cloth about 2.5 cm (1 in) less than this all round. You should aim at a circular or rectangular shape which will be large enough to slide easily on and off the object in question, without being too big. Now cut a rectangle of canvas long enough to go round the perimeter of the hole, plus 2–5 cm (1–2 in) to provide half that amount each end as a joining seam. Height of the rectangle should be sufficient to allow for the height of the item being covered, plus a seam allowance top and bottom. Join the two ends of the rectangle inside out, with a hand-sewn round seam (Fig. 3.4) and close off one end of the resulting box or cylinder by sewing a top piece in position, again with a round seam. Turn it right side out and seam it to the hole in the cover when you have mitre-cut into the corners; Fig. 7.5(a) and (b).

Windshield   If you need to fit the cover over a windshield, draw the plan outline onto the main cover, to match the plan view of the windshield shape; bridge any hollow as arrowed in Fig. 7.6(a). Much measurement and trial is needed, hopefully without too much error. Leave 7–8 cm (3 in) extra cloth all round for subsequent seaming with a small latitude for final fitting; this is especially important if you are working in cotton and have to turn the edges of cloth under to prevent fraying. Now cut a paper pattern which exactly fits the shape of the plexiglass plus its frame, with a mirror image folding along its top edge (this will also bridge any hollow along this line); Fig. 7.6(b). You will need to leave a wedge-shaped piece at either side to make the shaped join down the ends of the screen, so don't cut any paper away from here until you have offered the pattern to the boat. Staple the front of your pattern along the forward end of the aperture you have cut in the cover, and fold it over the windshield. You will need to cut a fair amount from the mirror image to make it fit the other side of the aperture, and you now also need to trim the side wedges to suit. Allow 2–3 cm (1 in) for joining, and then sew the cloth shape which you may happily cut from this pattern, using the round seaming stitch (Fig. 4.3) and working from the inside; Fig. 7.6(c).

Fig. 7.5 Boat cover – boots

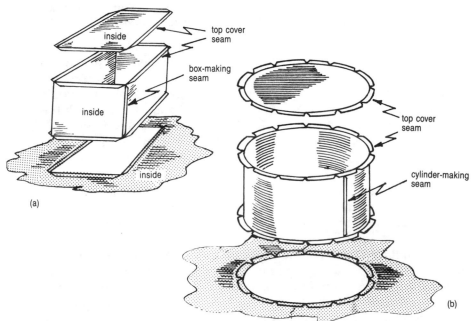

Most objects can be accommodated under a rectangular box-shaped boot; it should slide easily over the top (a). A cylindrical boot (b) may be thought better for a radome or a ventilator on a large boat.

Fig. 7.6 Boat cover – windshield

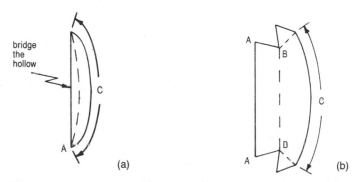

The aperture cut in the main cover should match the shape of the windshield when viewed from overhead, bridging any concave curves (a). Seam allowance has not been shown for the sake of clarity. The panel cut to fit the **front** slope of the screen should have a flap folding along the upper edge (b). Note that A-A on this panel must equal A-A in the aperture if it is to fit the gap; similarly, curve C on the panel should be the same length as curve C in the aperture. The top of the screen (B-B) may be the same as or shorter than A-A.

Final fitting

When you can place the cover on the boat so that it hangs more or less true, mark 5–10 cm (2–4 in) below the bottom of your planned overhangs, so that you have a level line all round. Trim to that line and the reason for a 15 cm (6 in) tabling allowance will become apparent; to get a straight and horizontal line, you will almost certainly have to cut off much more cloth in some places than in others. Sew your main tabling for one of the following treatments:

(a) A straight tabling for attaching various fasteners as discussed in Chapter 3;

(b) A hollow tabling right through, for fitting a drawstring;

(c) Trim the edge right back without a tabling, and reinforce with tape or webbing all round.

You may need to fit the cover round shrouds or stays or, indeed, a mast. You will have to provide a simple slit for this, with a lapped join fastened by one of the lacings we have already discussed; Figs. 3.15 or 3.16. If the cover has to fit round a mast, the slit for the forestay or for one of the shrouds will need to be taken right in to the mast, where a wrap-around collar along the lines of that for the sail cover of Fig. 7.2 will have to be incorporated.

The inner end of any slit for a stay is best reinforced with a circle of leather, or some stout equivalent, in the way of the wire to prevent chafe.

Sea Anchor

Design

The essence of a sea anchor is that it should be strong. With that in mind, this is best made almost entirely by hand (hand-sewing twine being so much stouter than machine thread). It will be roped all round (and down the sides), and will have a stout thimble at each end, with a light retrieval or tripping line attached aft. There is a cane hoop to keep the larger end open; Fig. 7.7.

Sizes Suggested measurements are given in the drawing (a) and (b) but, if you want to vary these, my illustration may still be used as a basic guide. The shape of the flat piece of canvas is reached in the way we examined for the mast coat, in the previous chapter; Fig. 6.7. You will almost certainly have to join two pieces of cloth to make this, so use the hand-sewn flat felled seam as described in Chapter 3; Fig. 3.6.

Materials Many sea anchors are still made of heavy (400 gm or 12 oz) cotton or even flax. But we don't want the bother of making sure that it isn't weakened by mildew caused by dampness, so we will use 200–300 gm (6–8 oz) polyester sailcloth. You will need 10m (33 ft) of 8–10 mm dia (1 in circ.) pre-stretched polyester rope, and a couple of thimbles to suit. Finally, a cane or ABS hoop of appropriate diameter.

Manufacture

Join the two sloping outer sides together, again using the flat felled seam, and you now have the basic cone. Wrap the hoop inside a fold of the larger end, and stitch it down with a tabling stitch; Fig. 3.7.

Roping

Form two rings of rope, with circumferences equal to the two ends of your canvas cone; these rings should both be long-spliced. Hand sew each to its appropriate end using the roping stitch of Fig. 3.11.

Draw four equidistant lines fore and aft, the length of the cone. Starting at the narrow end, and allowing a 7–8 cm (3 in) tail to hang loose, begin sewing the rope along one of these lines towards the wide end. When this is done, allow 120 cm (4 ft) of slack and sew back down the neighbouring pencil line (90 degrees round the cone) towards the narrow end. Allow 60 cm (2 ft) at that end and sew back along the side 180 degrees opposite to the second roping just completed; Fig. 7.7(a).

Pause now to fit the thimble at the apex of the first loop you made.

Fig. 7.7 Sea anchor

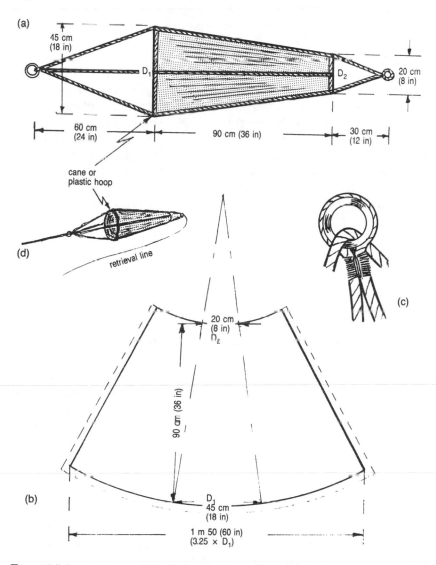

To establish the shape of the flat panel from which the basic cone is made, draw to scale the forward and aft diameters at the correct distance apart; D1 and D2 in (b). Project the sloping sides to their intersection and use this as the centre of concentric arcs through the ends of the two diameters; these arcs should be 3¼ times the diameters concerned (this is a similar construction to that of the mast coat in Fig. 6.7). The treatment of the forward thimble (before the two parts of the second rope loop are seized to those of the first) is shown in (c).

111

Pass the centre-point of the rope loop round the groove of the thimble, and seize the two parts of rope tightly together with the racking seizing of Fig. 5.7. Do the same at the narrow end.

The whole length of rope which you have not yet sewn is now passed *through* the first thimble and back to the final guide line drawn on the cone. It is important to ensure that all four spans are the same length, so that they share the pull of the anchor equally. Seize the two loose spans of rope right round the first seizing hard up against the thimble. Figure 7.7(c) shows this thimble before the second seizing is put on.

Sew the last length of rope back down to the narrow end, and cut it off with 7–8 cm (3 in) overlapping (as you did when starting). Sew both these short loose ends round the end of the canvas and back up the inside of the cone to give it strength. Attach a stout tow-rope forward and a light retrieval line to the thimble at the narrow end, and you are ready to hope that you never have to use it.

Bo'sun's Chair

Design

Bo'sun's chairs range from a simple bowline loop, or perhaps a plain board suspended from a pair of slings, to a shaped and padded 'soft-bottom' canvas seat fitted with foam rubber (see Jim Grant's book if you want to be pampered). The one illustrated at Fig. 7.8 is fairly quick to make, safe and adjustable.

Materials   A narrow strip of heavy 200–300 gm (6–8 oz) polyester forms the basic seat; a further strip makes a back strap; two lengths of 5 cm (2 in) webbing complete the canvas requirement. This is backed up by three 5 cm (2 in) stainless steel welded D-rings, a snap hook, and three small D-rings.

Manufacture

Cut the webbing with a hot knife to the lengths shown in Fig. 7.8(a); note the 7.5 cm (3 in) extra at each of the three ends, to be folded over to hold the three larger D-rings. Sew the shorter lengths of webbing at right angles to the longer piece, as shown. This sewing may be machined in a box-X pattern, provided you put in a few hand stitches as reinforcement (the D-rings will eventually be holding your weight aloft, so you need to be thorough).

The polyester is cut for the basic seat to the shape shown in Fig. 7.8(b). The adjustable back strap should only be tacked or stapled at this stage, until a fitting can be tried. Superimpose the seat on the webbing and sew together. Join the large D-rings in front of your chest and adjust the back strap for angle and basic length.

Fig. 7.8 Bo'sun's chair

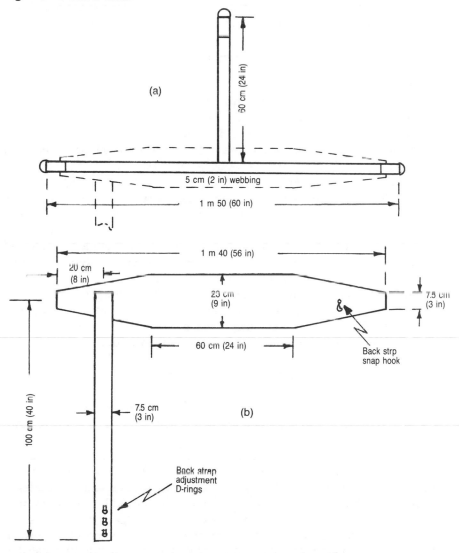

(a)

60 cm (24 in)

5 cm (2 in) webbing

1 m 50 (60 in)

1 m 40 (56 in)

20 cm
(8 in)

23 cm
(9 in)

7.5 cm
(3 in)

60 cm (24 in)

Back strp
snap hook

7.5 cm
(3 in)

(b)

100 cm (40 in)

Back strap
adjustment
D-rings

The basic webbing skeleton is best hand sewn for strength (a). The polyester flesh is put onto these bones as shown in (b), and it will be noted that the ends of canvas fall short of the D-rings sewn to the webbing, by a small amount.

The small D-rings are sewn on narrow tabs as in Fig. 3.17, to mate with a snap hook on the opposite side of the seat (put it on the outside for comfort). You may add a pocket for tools if you wish. It is better to have a fully enclosed pocket (with velcro) rather than a few loops of webbing through which tools may be pushed like six-guns; a spanner or screwdriver dropped from aloft can do as much damage as a six-gun.

Awnings

Design

I can't of course tell you exactly how to make an awning for your boat, for it would be the wrong size. What I can do, however, is to explain the principles and advise on one or two points of contention. At the outset, let me say that I have borrowed ideas from various boats I have seen, and also from Lin and Larry Pardey's thoughts on *Serrafyn's* awnings, and from Jim Grant, who has some wise words to say in his book; Fig. 7.9.

The Pardeys make the point that you should keep your awning simple to operate, particularly to unship in a hurry, and it will then be regularly used. You will agree with this the first time you are suddenly blown from your idyllic anchorage towards a lee shore, and need to handle your ground tackle in a hurry and have a good view from the cockpit at the same time. More specific design points worth listing include:

(a) Restrict the awning's coverage to aft of the mast for ease of rigging;
(b) Don't have integral side curtains for the same reason; they also tend to cut down cooling breezes;
(c) Try to do without battens; they are clumsy and, if made of wood, will eventually break;
(d) Have permanently attached guys at each corner (slip knots make for a quick take-down). Intermediate lacing eyelets enable you to pull down one side against the glare of the setting sun;
(e) Velcro allows easy attachment of side screens, or of mosquito netting if necessary (weight the bottom of netting to hold it down).

Materials   Assuming that the awning will be used in tropical waters, and hopefully exposed to long periods of ultraviolet rays, there is much to be said for cotton; it will last well, and is waterproof if you are suddenly caught in a shower. If you make a small one, it should be strong enough to be turned into a make-shift windbreak or spray dodger for the helmsman in blustery weather. Nylon, of course, is easy to stow and easy to work (the cheapest sewing machine will make light of it, and nylon heat seals); it also comes in a wide range of colours. PVC-coated polyester or nylon resists sunlight, but can be bulky to stow; if you have that sort of space, you will get a better-looking job from acrylic.

Fig. 7.9 Awnings

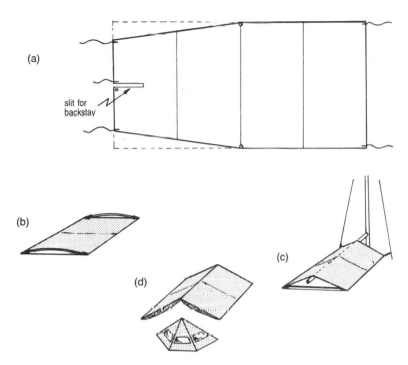

An awning may be rectangular as shown in the dashed outline in (a), or else shaped to fit the stern better (hard outline); there may or may not be a need for a slit for the backstay or topping lift. The battens in (b) are under compression in pockets on top of the awning; those in (c) are tied into pockets underneath, to form gable ends. the awning at (d) has an inner nylon lining acting as insulation, and the principles of the endpiece with windows are shown.

Manufacture

To get both length and width sufficient for a decent awning, you will probably need to join at least two cloths. A flat felled seam (Fig. 4.4) is watertight, and is best taken across the awning so that any water will run off along the seam; use double-sided sticky tape when seaming, to stop creep of one cloth on the other.

Tablings   Allow wide tablings (5 cm or 2 in) to give good holding for the lacings and eyes.

Battens   If you must have battens to spread your awning, get some light alloy or fibreglass tent poles which take apart into sections. These may be fitted into 10–15 cm (4–6 in) wide sleeves at the forward and aft ends (they remain open at each end). If you also need a batten across the middle, sew a wide piece of material or webbing to the underside of the awning. Battens may be rigged across the top by bending them to fit into reinforced webbing pockets on top of the awning; Fig. 7.9(b). Or you may fit them into rings or pockets to act as 'gable ends'; Fig. 7.9(c).

Support   In a sailing boat, the weight of the awning will usually be taken by the main boom suspended by its topping lift; if the awning extends aft of the boom end, you will need either to cut a small opening to thread the topping lift, or else to slit the awning all the way aft, using velcro or lacing to close it off. A large awning with no main boom support (for a motor cruiser) may need a rope sewn all along the ridge, so that weight may be taken by the rope without straining the material. Fold the awning in half lengthways, insides touching. Lay a length of prestretched polyester rope (6–8 mm dia or ³/₄–1 in circ) inside the fold, with enough at each end for a spliced attachment eye. Machine as close as you can get (a zipper foot attachment will help here), or machine a light messenger line in place and then draw the rope through afterwards. Splice an eye each end, leaving the rope to 'float' freely in its channel (if you have any batten sleeves crossing this rope, they will have to be made in two halves).

Fixings   Hand sewn rings (Fig. 3.10) will repay the extra work involved by lasting longer than punched eyelets. If you need sleeves for poles, you will have to make sure that the tabling doesn't block them by being sewn right across; you might be better off with tab rings as shown in Fig. 2.4.

Extras   I can't think that you will go to all this trouble to keep the sun off, and then want to put in a window to let it back again. But it is just possible that you may fit an end cloth, and then decide that you want to see out fore or aft (when making an end cloth attachment, always make a paper pattern first, tape or pin it in place, and then trim until you have a good fit); window procedure is described in Fig. 6.14. Equally, you may want to line your awning with light nylon to increase its insulation effect. Sew the inside panel along the ridge of the main awning and at the eaves, to reduce danger of a tangle when folding away. If you make the inner lining just that little bit wider than the top cover, it will hang down slightly in use and create an air space for the insulation you seek; Fig. 7.9(d).

Spinnaker Strangler

Design

There are many names for imitations of the Spee Squeezer®, which was invented by Chris Hall at Cowes back in the late 1960s (Spinnaker Sally, the Spiral, Dowser and Snuffer are but a few), so I don't see why I shouldn't introduce my own word. If somebody, somewhere along the line, has already called their product a Strangler, I can but tender my apologies.

I have often wanted to strangle that sail when I was on the foredeck, so this is as good a name as any.

What a wonderful idea Chris had! It must stand alongside Philip Benson's turtle, for taking much of the hassle out of launching the spinnaker – and this one also recovers it; some of them can even be used as a crude form of reefing. This DIY version will last reasonably well, the weak point (if any) being the funnel; Fig. 7.10.

Materials   You need a length of spinnaker nylon as long as the height of the spinnaker; width should be sufficient to fit round the funnel you use – 75 cm (2 ft 6 in) should be enough, so you will want a full width of cloth (ask you sailmaker if he has a reject). You may either buy a special funnel from your local sail loft, or make one from a plastic bucket; these instructions show you how to modify a bucket, which should be a robust one. You will need a small swivel block with becket, a couple of shackles, a short length of polythene tubing (equal to the height of your funnel/bucket), enough polyester tape or webbing to go twice round the funnel, an uphaul/downhaul 6–8 mm dia. ($^3/_4$–1 in circ.) equal in length to just over twice the height of the spinnaker, and half a dozen small rings to act as fairleads for the uphaul.

Manufacture

Making the Strangler is clean and easy; it may be undertaken in the living room, with confidence that it will not unduly disturb the even running of the household (but I take no responsibility if it does).

Funnel   Form the funnel by cutting the bottom off the bucket on the slant, with the apex opposite one of the handle attachments; Fig. 7.10(a). Smooth the raw edge carefully, and remove the handle. You now need an attachment point for the uphaul at this apex, and another for the downhaul at the lower end, preferably at the reinforced part where the handle was attached. These attachments are best achieved by punched eyelets, fitting a couple of reinforcing washers at the weaker apex (uphaul), made from some of the plastic which you cut from the bucket, if they can be accommodated.

Sleeve   Turn the length of nylon into a tube, to fit exactly round the narrow end of the funnel; it should taper slightly (by about a third) in the upper quarter. Sew half a dozen rings at equal intervals down the inside of the sleeve (along the seam for added strength) leading to the attachment point at the funnel apex.

Pulley system   Your pulley needs to fit into the head of the sleeve, on a strop about equal in length to the height of the funnel; this is to allow the head of the spinnaker to deploy when it is full of wind, without pressing on the sides of the funnel. To give it some rigidity, this strop is best led through a length of plastic hose. At its top end there should be a spliced eye to attach to the becket of the pulley; its lower end also has a spliced eye (made *after* the polythene tubing has been fitted over the rope), for attaching to the head of the spinnaker; Fig. 7.10(b).

Fig. 7.10 Spi strangler

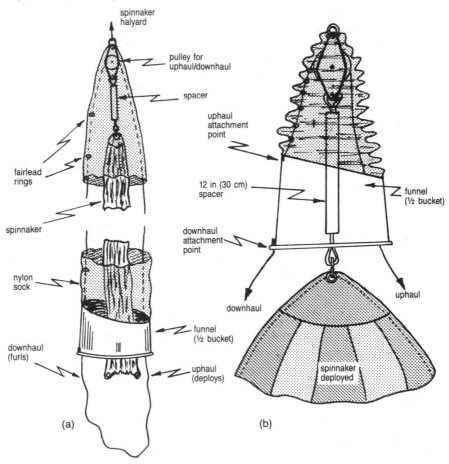

The principles of the Strangler are clearly shown in (a). The head is shown in some detail at (b), which is drawn with the funnel aloft. Note the spacer strop in a short plastic tube, designed to allow the head of the spinnaker to hang below the funnel when it is deployed. If you have trouble with the uphaul/downhaul jamming, try running the line through a similar length of tubing lashed to the pulley, so that it clears the concertina of nylon when the funnel is hard up.

Assembly

Reeve the uphaul/downhaul through the block. Gather the top of the sleeve round the top of the pulley, and hand sew it to the becket between the pulley and its shackle, so that the pulley hangs down inside the sleeve with its strop below it (b). You may find that you need a second strop here, to provide enough space for the bunch of nylon to gather round the top. Reeve the free end of one fall of the uphaul/downhaul through the small ring fairleads inside the sleeve, down to the eyelet at the narrow end of the funnel, where it should be attached.

The sleeve is now hand sewn to the narrow end of the funnel, so that it is attached all round, preferably with reinforcing tape covering each side as you sew. Make sure that the joining seam down the length of the sleeve lies in a straight line without twists, so that the ring fairleads run true to the funnel apex.

Attach the other free end of the uphaul/downhaul to the lower (wider) end of the funnel, and you are ready to load your spinnaker.

Loading

Ensure that the two leeches of the spinnaker are clear and free from twists. Shackle the head to the lower end of the strop inside the sleeve. The funnel is then pulled down over the spinnaker, bringing the sleeve with it, as the uphaul/downhaul renders round the pulley.

Like this book, the whole thing is now finished and ready to be put to good use.

Bibliography

Blandford, Percy W. *Modern Sailmaking*, Tab Books, USA 1979

Blandford, Percy W. *Working in Canvas*, Brown Son & Ferguson, UK 1965

Coats, J. & P. Ltd. *The Technology of Thread Seams*, Industrial Products Marketing, UK 1985

Grant, Jim. *The Complete Canvas Worker's Guide*, International Marine Publishing Co., USA 1986, and Ashford Press Publishing, UK 1986

Howard-Williams, Jeremy. *The Care and Repair of Sails*, 2nd Edition, Adlard Coles Ltd, UK 1985, and Hearst Marine Books, USA 1985

Howard-Williams, Jeremy. *Sails*, 6th Edition, Adlard Coles Ltd, UK 1988, and John de Graff, USA 1989

Howard-Williams, Jeremy. *Small Boat Sails*, 3rd Edition, Adlard Coles Ltd, UK 1987, and Sheridan House Inc., USA 1987

ICI Fibres. *Laundering and Dry Cleaning Terylene Sails*, Privately Printed in UK

Rosenow, Frank. *The Ditty Bag Book*, Sail Books Inc, USA 1976, and Adlard Coles Ltd, UK 1976

Schmit, Bill. *Sailmaking Made Easy*, Water, Wind and Sail Publications USA, 1974

Index